The Right Color

EVE ASHCRAFT
COLOR
THE
ESSENTIAL
PALETTE
28 COLORS

The Right Color

Eve Ashcraft

with Heather Smith MacIsaac

ARTISAN · NEW YORK

Published by Artisan
A division of Workman Publishing
Company, Inc.
225 Varick Street
New York, NY 10014-4381
www.artisanbooks.com

Published simultaneously in Canada by
Thomas Allen & Son, Limited

Library of Congress Cataloging-in-
Publication Data
 The right color / Eve Ashcraft with
Heather Smith MacIsaac.
   p. cm.
 Includes bibliographical references.
 ISBN-978-1-57965-408-5
1. Color in interior decoration. I. MacIsaac,
Heather Smith. II. Title.
 NK2115.5.C6A84 2011
 747'.94—dc22   2010050764

Design by Jan Derevjanik

Printed in Singapore
First printing, October 2011

10 9 8 7 6 5 4 3 2 1

Additional Photography Credits

William Abranowicz/Art + Commerce: pages 31, 33, 35, 37, 41 (below), 42, 45, 48–49, 51, 53, 58, 59 (above), 60 (right), 61, 69, 71, 72 (below), 73 (left), 77–78, 84 (above), 85 (above), 87, 88 (above), 89 (above), 91–92, 93 (right), 96, 97 (below), 99 (above), 101, 102 (above), 103 (above), 105–6, 107 (below), 109, 110 (above), 111 (below), 113 (above), 116 (below), 117 (above), and 119 (below)

Fernando Bengoechea: page 39

Paul Costello: pages 83, 128–29, and 131–33

David Gilbert: pages 34, 93 (left), and 97 (above)

Mark Huddleston: page 125

Interior Archive: page 36: Christopher Simon Sykes; pages 43, 73 (right), 107 (above), and 116 (above): Eric Piasecki; pages 50, 54, and 79: Fritz von der Schulenburg; page 59 (below): Alex Ramsay; pages 60 (below left), 62, 66–67, 75, 76 (right), 111 (above), and 113 (below): Simon Upton; pages 63 and 74: Jacques Dirand; page 68: Helen Fickling; page 88 (below): Jean-Marc Palisse; page 110 (below): Simon Maxwell

iStock: pages 7 (above left, below center, and below right), 8, 9 (left), 41 (above), and 76 (left)

Åke E:son Lindman: pages 122–24 and 126–27

Redcover: page 46: Peter Margonelli; page 47: James Mitchell; pages 57, 70, and 117 (below): Ken Hayden; page 72 (above): Henry Wilson; page 89 (below): Keith Scott Morton; page 102 (below): Christopher Drake

Gil Schafer: pages 130 and 146

Victor Schrager: pages vi, 2, 4, 28, and 209 (right)

Fritz von der Schulenburg: pages 27 and 85 (below)

Jonathan Wallen: page 115

Contents

Introduction

Lots of people have asked me how I got involved in such a specific and, in their minds, difficult line of work. I did not set out to become a color expert, although I have been immersed in color my whole life, going back to my Michigan childhood. My mother was a painter with no fear of color. Always comfortable with her own ideas and methods, she spent many evenings spread out on our living

room floor, palette in one hand, brush in the other, glass of red wine and ashtray at her side. Family friends and, later, clients wanted affordable art with a capital *A* to hang in their Bloomfield Hills living rooms, so she made copies of famous paintings by Sir Joshua Reynolds and Thomas Gainsborough. With a little luck, I'd be allowed to watch in awe as her quick brush collected bits of cadmium yellow and French yellow ochre and a smidge of raw umber to make a glinting brass button for Captain Robert Orme's coat in her version of the Reynolds portrait. Dabs of titanium white and French yellow ochre with a pinch of red oxide became the tiny champagne pearls of the magnificent luminous rope that hung like an anchor around Mrs. Siddons's neck in my mother's interpretation of Reynolds's *Mrs. Siddons as the Tragic Muse.*

In our house, color wasn't something to worry or even wonder about—it was something to do. In contrast to my friends' beige living rooms, ours had canary-yellow walls and Chippendale chairs with fuchsia silk cushions. Our home was vibrant and bold, perhaps unusual to others, but normal to me. Consequently I didn't understand just how unnerving color could be for many people. By the time I went to college I was armed with an innate confidence and a tireless curiosity about what could be done with color. Although I started off as

a photography major, I ended up training as a fine art painter. Art school and apprenticeships gave me practical and technical skills that refined my natural interest in color. With greater frequency, people asked me to help them pick out the right hues—for walls, clothes, art projects, advertisements, even typefaces. I loved looking at all the factors that went into making color choices. Without consciously planning for it, I had found my career as a color specialist.

Over the last twenty years, my work on color-related projects has taken me to all regions of the country, to houses, apartments, boardrooms, labs, architecture firms, photography studios, retail shops, galleries, and artists' studios. And though the locations may vary, the issues are often closely related. Color can be a mysterious, even daunting world unto itself, and many people are relieved to entrust color choices to someone who lives and works in that world every day. Unlike an architect or an interior designer, who is immersed in all the complexities of a major project, I focus on a narrow slice, which allows for a deeper investigation and imagining of just one facet: color. Despite being carefully thought out, my work is often unobtrusive, whether it's choosing the colors of the walls of a neutral but pleasing living room in Greenwich, Connecticut, or of the interiors of the Armani Casa store in New York's SoHo. (Giorgio

Armani's architects called me in to adjust a wall color—a pale stone gray—that struck just the right note in fog-prone Milan but flattened in New York's harder light.)

On the other end of the color spectrum, but no less challenging, I was called in to "rescue" several Burger King restaurants in New York City by coming up with an updated palette that would coordinate with the chain's signature bright orange and yellow plastic. For example, in one

location I painted the walls a combination of blue lapis and marigold yellow. (Later the owner hired me to choose colors for his ultramodern New York City high-rise apartment; I put hot-pink accents in his foyer in an otherwise stark white urban pad.) I've been asked to find a color for Banana Republic watch faces (it had to be just the right tone of cream . . . not as easy as it sounds) and worked with the photographer Richard Avedon to select the red and blue typefaces on several of his book covers. I've produced all kinds of custom-colored backgrounds for use in product photography. You've probably seen my work in advertisements for Godiva chocolates and Tiffany & Co. jewelry, as well as in catalogs for Saks Fifth Avenue, Nordstrom, Gucci, Ralph Lauren, Garnet Hill, Eileen Fisher, and Victoria's Secret. I've made sets and colorful backdrops for photo shoots in such magazines as *Vanity Fair, Vogue, Martha Stewart Living, Food & Wine, This Old House,* and *The New Yorker.* And in what has to be the oddest request I've ever received, one client asked me to help choose the right white for her dental veneers!

My work has taken me through many doors and left me staring at the walls, which proved very helpful when Martha Stewart asked me to collaborate on developing her first two paint lines—Araucana Colors and Everyday Colors. It was the opportunity of a lifetime. Martha has a keen eye and a brilliant sense of color, not to mention an extraordinary collection of beautiful and fascinating objects, furniture, and ephemera from which to draw inspiration. For the initial collection, Araucana Colors, we found our palette in the henhouse, in the subtle blues and greens of the eggs of

Martha's Araucana chickens. The scope of this enormous undertaking, creating a curated collection of colors for the home, was pioneering at the time. For me, it was a deeply satisfying enterprise.

Much of my work has focused on residential interiors for my wonderful private clientele. Domestic spaces can be the most challenging of all color projects because they are so loaded with hopes, dreams, and associations, yet also must be functional. Often new clients will arrive on my studio doorstep after a phone call in which they sheepishly admit to standing frozen in a sea of paint samples, unable to decide which color is the "right" one for their living room or hallway. More than once, a caller has said that he doesn't even know exactly what I "do" but that his dearest friend insisted he call me and explain his dilemma. The actor Rick Moranis did precisely this—contacted me in a panic because his living room had been painted the color of a banana peel (not so funny, it seems, even for a comedian) and beseeched me to rescue his home by doing whatever it is that I do. He got my number from Steve Martin, for whom I had just created a calm linen-white envelope as the backdrop for the amazing art collection in his Central Park West apartment.

Not all of my clients are famous. Most are "normal" people like us, if normal means somehow believing that if you look at a wall long enough, the right color will simply emerge. There's no escaping the exciting yet challenging fact that color is intensely personal and can be so enmeshed with context and memory that it often takes an impartial yet trained eye to settle on just the right hue. Like a designer or a decorator, I initially spend a lot of time with clients, collecting information about how they live, what inspires and moves them, what colors they like and dislike and have meaningful memories of, what kind of atmosphere they want their homes to have. The goal is to create an environment that uses color to support and enhance both their needs and their desires.

Although this book deals with the comparatively narrow world of how to use color in our homes, its principles for building a vital relationship with color have a much broader application.

This book is more than an invitation to be a guest at a colorful party; it's an inspiration to throw the party yourself. Not only is *The Right Color* filled with all I have learned from working directly with color and paint for more than twenty years, it is also intended to be a literal eye-opener. There are ideas and answers on every page, but more than that, I offer and advocate a holistic method—a way of learning to see color in context.

I chose the title *The Right Color* because that's what my clients are always searching for: the perfect hue. It's my hope that this book will guide you to finding your palette. It will show you the how and why of color and, more important, help you discover who you are in relation to color, because that is ultimately the only way to find the right colors for you.

1

A BRIEF HISTORY OF COLOR

Today we can walk into a paint store, walk out with virtually any color we want, and change our home in an afternoon. Although ready-mixed paints have been around for more than a century, the endless spectrum of color made possible by modern technology is relatively new.

While our choices have multiplied, our ability to choose has not improved. I've received countless calls from stressed-out homeowners who have run aground mid-renovation, unable to select another switch-plate cover, let alone a wall color. Add to that the common perception that the wrong decision can derail a project, causing untold anxiety and expense. In this part of the book, I'm going to show you how to make decisions about color. In many ways, you already have these skills. You start your day making color choices: You add milk to your coffee until it's just the right shade of brown. You coordinate your clothing, mixing and matching colors until the balance seems right. Even in the car on your way to work, you take cues from color—you stop at red and go with green. Don't underestimate your ability to choose a color; you're processing colors all the time. What follows in this chapter is information about color—its history, its composition, how it is perceived—that I hope will enlighten, amuse, and, above all, inspire you.

Color Through the Ages

When I started out as a painter, I had no idea how privileged we are today to have at our fingertips almost any color at a relatively affordable cost. For centuries, color—and the pigments to create it—was as precious as gold. Imagine if I, as a color expert, held the secret formula to the perfect sky-blue paint and, to my colleagues' chagrin, only my clients could have access to that hue for their walls.

This kind of scarcity and level of secrecy was once common in the world of color. Artists would go to great lengths to protect and keep secret their color formulations. Costly pigments were held under lock and key. Even the most prominent artists relied on wealthy patrons to front them the money to procure expensive pigments. For example, if Vermeer had a client who commissioned a painting containing a certain amount of costly ultramarine blue, that patron would have to advance the money so the artist could buy the precise amount of the pigment needed. And Vermeer would have to accept visits from financial auditors who would make sure that the pigment was being used as contracted (and that none was being squirreled away by the artist or his helpers).

If you have ever felt superficial in obsessing about your home's palette, consider this: you are hardwired to do so. From the beginning of time, people have relied on color to create and shape their environments. Early humans, not content to use only charred wood to draw pictures of animals on the walls of their caves, devised a way to make three additional colors to enhance their paintings. They discovered that by grinding chunks of earth to extract white, yellow, and red pigments, they could make their drawings a whole lot more dynamic. What follows is a highly subjective timeline featuring important moments in color history from prehistoric to modern times.

Vermeer's *Girl with a Pearl Earring* features his masterful use of lead-tin yellow paired with ultramarine blue.

30,000 Years of Color

30,000 BC
The earliest recorded color scheme—red, yellow, white, and black—is used by Paleolithic cave dwellers in Chauvet Cave, located in what is now southern France, who created pigments from ochre clay, white chalk, and charcoal. The three-color palette suffices for about 25,000 years.

5000
At last the color palette expands. Egyptians create new shades by grinding such stones as lapis lazuli (blue) and malachite (green), as well as pure gold, which is used to embellish objects and images.

3000
Colored glass recipes, recorded in cuneiform, are produced by the Mesopotamians. The techniques change very little and are used to make the stained glass of the Middle Ages 4,000 years later.

2500
Egyptians create the first synthetic pigment, known as Alexandrian or Egyptian blue, using copper and calcium.

438
In its final stages of completion, the Parthenon receives an opulent paint job, reflecting the Grecian appetite for color. Centuries of rain wash the vibrant colors off the marble, falsely establishing the iconic white temple as a true reflection of ancient Greek sensibility.

330
Aristotle writes that the four elements—fire, earth, water, and air—are represented by color, and not the ones we have come to expect: fire = white, earth = black, water = yellow, and air = red.

200
Wealthy Romans take a fancy to cinnabar, an earthy red made from a prohibitively expensive pigment ground from a quartz-like stone. Convicts are enlisted to mine the toxic, mercury-laden rock, which is imported from such places as Spain and Egypt.

25
Cleopatra wears pure ground lapis lazuli as eye shadow.

AD 1
In Pompeii, the importance of interior decoration reaches unprecedented heights. Villa dwellers display their wealth with cinnabar-frescoed walls costing a year's wages.

60
Only the Roman emperor, Nero, is permitted to wear purple, a color derived from mollusk secretions. Death is the penalty for lawbreakers.

100
There are over seventy Latin terms for color, a dramatic increase from Homer's time (the Greek poet used just five).

410
Rome is sacked. The fall of the Empire begins. Much sophisticated knowledge about color production is lost.

600
In Ravenna, Italy, Byzantine mosaics of shimmering glass tiles, or tesserae, are produced in a rainbow of translucent colors.

1100
The first known written version of "Little Red Riding Hood" is penned. Many see the red hood as a symbol for danger and the wolf as the devil.

1200
Stained-glass windows are common and richly colored. Clear glass is the most difficult to produce. The French "recycle" ancient Roman glass vessels and mosaic tiles as a means to produce blue glass.

1347
The Black Death (bubonic plague) sweeps Europe for three hellish years.

1360
Black is in fashion in Europe, reflecting the dark mood after the plague. Sumptuary laws of the time restrict the luxury and ostentation associated with brightly colored textiles; only wealthy citizens are permitted to wear fine fabrics in rich colors.

1400
During the fifteenth century, European cities use color-coded clothing to identify undesirable, infirm, dangerous, and outcast people. Red is assigned to prostitutes, green to idiots, yellow to heretics. Only blue escapes this lowly task and is never used to mark a person with shame.

1467
Pope Paul II decrees cochineal red as the color for cardinals' robes, dethroning purple. Cochineal red is made from tiny Mexican beetles and continues to be used today as a food dye.

1508
Michelangelo begins painting the ceiling of the Sistine Chapel, using an unprecedented range of colors, including bright red, apple green, and deep orange.

1525
German peasants revolt against local laws, demanding the right to wear red clothing.

1529
The term *red tape* originates from the huge pile of annulment petitions—bound in red ribbon—submitted to Pope Clement VII by Henry VIII in his desperate attempt to annul his marriage to Catherine of Aragon.

1609
France bans indigo imports from India, permitting only the native (and much less effective) blue dye made from the indigenous herb woad. Anyone breaking the law faces a death sentence. Indigo later prevails, and it is still used today.

1635
Paint makers and housepainters, former members of the English guild system, bring their skills to the American colonies. Trade secrets hold until the nineteenth century, when paint is no longer handmade.

1637
René Descartes outlines the science of the rainbow. The mnemonic "Richard of York gave battle in vain" is created to help students remember the seven colors of the arc: red, orange, yellow, green, blue, indigo, and violet.

1643
The Sun King, Louis XIV, begins his reign in France. The French court at Versailles becomes the center of fashion. Pastel silks flow through its grand halls.

1653
The Taj Mahal is completed. The white stone exterior reflects pink as the sun sets.

1664
Anglo-Irish chemist Robert Boyle names the three primary colors that we recognize today—red, blue, and yellow.

1665
Vermeer paints *Girl with a Pearl Earring*. It features his masterful use of lead-tin yellow paired with ultramarine blue. The pigment is so costly that Vermeer does not use the color until it is paid for on commission.

1666
By sending a slim ray of white light through a glass prism, Sir Isaac Newton determines the irreducible colors of the spectrum.

1667
John Smith writes the widely used painter's manual *The Art of Painting*. British housepainters now have an indispensable guide to techniques and materials.

1704
Newton writes *Opticks*, in which he combines primary and secondary colors to form the color wheel. He associates his seven basic colors—violet, indigo, blue, green, yellow, orange, and red—with the seven tones of the diatonic music scale.

1730
Polka-dotted kitchen ceilings appear in early American homes. The spots are made with a simple brush twist of lampblack over whitewash.

1750
White becomes the most popular exterior color for American buildings.

1768
Thomas Jefferson begins work on his Virginia home, Monticello. Completed in 1808, its South Square room has black plaster walls, and the entry hall has grass-green-painted floors topped with a band of yellow on the walls between the baseboard and the chair rail.

1776
Though cochineal red helps to cover the bloodstains on the uniforms of British soldiers during the Revolutionary War, it makes the infamous redcoats easy targets. The same red dye is used by the British army until 1952.

1790s
Dark green becomes a popular exterior trim color in the United States. Verdigris, or deep fine green, is popular for libraries and dining rooms in British Georgian homes. Derived from expensive pigment, the color conveys taste and social status.

1800
Clad in limestone, the White House in Washington, D.C., perpetuates the myth that ancient classical architecture was white.

1810
In *Theory of Colours*, Johann Wolfgang von Goethe hopes to leave behind a valuable treatise of scientific merit, but the lasting power of his work lies in his perception of color as subjective and cultural.

1828
French chemist Jean-Baptiste Guimet unlocks the formula for a synthetic blue to rival lapis lazuli. Known as French ultramarine, its affordability puts the color within everyone's reach.

1831
Charles Darwin takes botanical artist Patrick Syme's *Werner's Nomenclature of Colours* on his five-year-long HMS *Beagle* voyage. He uses Syme's terminology to describe the color of an octopus as "a tint between a hyacinth red and a chestnut-brown."

1842
Charles Dickens visits Worcester, Massachusetts, observing that "all the buildings looked as if they had been painted that morning . . . every house is the whitest of white; every Venetian blind the greenest of green."

1850
In *The Architecture of Country Homes*, American architect Andrew Jackson Downing states that white "is too glaring and conspicuous. We scarcely know anything more uncomfortable to the eye . . . it is absolutely painful."

1853
In California, Levi Strauss makes the first indigo-dyed blue jeans and sells them to gold miners.

1861
Prince Albert dies, and Queen Victoria begins her lifelong practice of wearing nothing but black. Once colorful doors and railings throughout the British Empire are painted black in sympathy. Ninety percent of doors and railings in Britain remain black.

1870
The industrial revolution gives birth to the modern paint industry: machines to grind pigments and mix paints are invented, railroads move products greater distances, and more sophisticated printing presses usher in paint company color cards and brochures.

1874
The British post office stops painting mailboxes green because people are bumping into them. They switch to red.

1879
Thomas Edison patents his lightbulb. Soon all interior spaces will be lit with electric fixtures.

1885
American paint company Sherwin-Williams publishes *What Color?* for consumers faced with a new problem: too many choices.

1888
Vincent van Gogh shocks the art world with the dissonant, deliberately contrasting palette of *The Night Café:* glowing yellow lights, bloodred walls, a green ceiling, and a yellow floor.

1901
Picasso enters his Blue Period following the suicide of a friend.

1903
The Crayola crayon box makes its debut with eight colors: red, orange, yellow, green, blue, violet, brown, and black. It sells for a nickel.

1904
Nobel Prize–winning English physicist John Strutt, aka Lord Rayleigh, discovers the phenomenon now known as Rayleigh scattering. It explains why the sky is blue.

1905
The Yellow Cab Co. is founded in New York, research having determined that yellow is the color most easily seen from a distance.

1914
The Ford Motor Company builds cars so quickly that only japan black paint will

dry fast enough to keep the assembly lines going at full speed, prompting Henry Ford's famous remark: "Any color . . . so long as it is black."

1919
Walter Gropius founds the Bauhaus. Josef Albers, Johannes Itten, and Wassily Kandinsky teach color and painting courses. The Bauhaus methods greatly influence all subsequent art and color education.

1926
Coco Chanel debuts the "little black dress," revolutionizing fashion.

1941
Chocolate M&M's debut in their original candy-coated palette of orange, yellow, brown, red, green, and violet.

1945
Organizers of the newly formed United Nations choose white and blue, "the opposite of red, the color of war," as its official colors.

1949
Following the Maoist revolution, all Chinese citizens must wear blue clothing.

1950
Josef Albers begins his twenty-six-year painting and color project "Homage to the Square." He produces over 1,000 works.

1954
The American stop sign is standardized to a red background with white letters. It had previously been red on yellow and, before that, white on black.

1958
French artist Yves Klein commissions chemists to create his famous signature color, IKB—International Klein Blue. Because it is outside the color gamut of computer displays, IKB is impossible to accurately replicate on the screen.

1963
Josef Albers publishes *Interaction of Color,* which becomes the seminal text on color theory.

Lawrence Herbert invents the Pantone matching system to standardize colors throughout the printing industry.

1966
The Rolling Stones release their song "Paint It, Black." This is followed a year later by Procol Harum's "A Whiter Shade of Pale."

1978
Lead—long used as an ingredient in paint—is banned for residential use in the United States following the discovery that lead exposure can be toxic, especially to children.

1987
In bringing attention to the burgeoning AIDS health crisis, the activist group ACT UP cements the

right-side-up pink triangle as a symbol of gay rights protest. Later, in the 1990s, pink in the form of a looped ribbon will draw awareness to another health issue: breast cancer.

1994
The Paleolithic masterpieces in the Chauvet Cave are discovered in the Ardèche Valley in France. The 30,000-year-old images are so stunning that the discovery is thought to be a hoax.

1998
Ubiquitous beige computers are upstaged by Apple's eye-catching iMac desktops in translucent candy colors.

2004
The Lance Armstrong Foundation distributes yellow silicone wristbands as a fund-raising tool for cancer research. The bracelet's color is inspired by the hue of the jersey won by the leader of the Tour de France.

2006
The word *green* becomes synonymous with the growing environmental movement.

2008
The American presidential election is a color-coded battle with the country split between "red" and "blue" states. Barack Obama is the first person of color to be elected president of the United States.

The Color Wheel

I suppose no book on color would be complete without the color wheel; you expect to see it. But in all honesty, it's not what I turn to when choosing a palette, because I think it oversimplifies the infinite possibilities of color choice. Yet color, like language, does have a basic structure that is helpful to know. The simple color wheel composed of six wedges is an organizational tool long used to present color in its most basic state: three primary colors—red, yellow, and blue, which are hues that cannot be made from other colors—and three secondary colors—orange, green, and purple, each one the result of mixing two primary colors together (red mixed with yellow makes orange, and so on).

Where colors sit on the wheel helps us understand how they work. Analogous colors are ones that sit next to one another, like yellow and green, and are harmonious when used together. Complementary colors sit directly across from each other on the wheel, like green and red or orange and blue, creating much more dynamic and stimulating color combinations. Color temperature is also illustrated in a basic way on the wheel, with cool colors occupying one half of the wheel and warm colors the other.

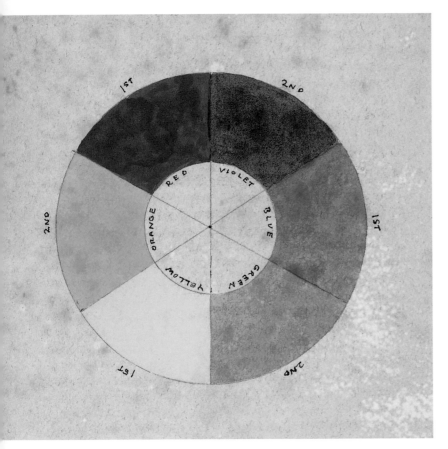

My rendering of the basic color wheel, painted on a page taken from a book printed in 1810, the same year Goethe's *Theory of Colours* was published.

The Science of Color

Believe it or not, color perception starts in the womb, where we begin to detect light about three months before we are born. Our eyes are composed of millions of sensitive nerve endings working tirelessly to absorb and relay information. Every eye has two kinds of photoreceptors, rods and cones, which respond to light and send signals to the brain. That is how we "see."

Without light, we are essentially color-blind. We see a color when an object's surface absorbs all the hues in the visible spectrum except the one we see. The magnificent mineral lapis lazuli is blue because blue is what is being reflected; equally, a fire engine looks red because that is the color that is not being absorbed. This is because light activates surfaces. The more available light, the more color we see; conversely, if there is no light at all, there is also no color, at least to our eyes. (Amazingly, some animals and insects can see parts of the spectrum that are invisible to the human eye.)

Here is an experiment: Direct your eyes to the nearest wall. Is its color uniform? Chances are, the wall's hue consists of several subtle variations of one color. This is due to variations in the intensity of the light hitting the wall, which could be caused by a passing cloud, perhaps, or the shadow of a tree outside a window.

The Language of Color

I once had a client ask that I not use "pink" to describe the color she had chosen for a bathroom. Not in front of her husband, at any rate, since he was not the kind of man who could abide anything pink in his home. I asked whether she thought he might find the words *salmon* and *melon* more appealing. These terms swiftly became the approved descriptions, and the pink paint went on the couple's walls.

We tend to use the names of common objects to describe and distinguish colors. If I say simply "red," you at least know that I'm not talking about blue. But if I say "fire-engine red" or "Coke-can red," you have a much clearer image of the color I'm describing. When I work with color in my studio, I don't think about mixing Coke can with fire engine. I think about using various pigments to tone or tint, deepen or lighten, or push the red in the direction of another color, like brown or purple. Because of my work, I think of color as the sum of its pigments—like combining cadmium red medium with raw umber and purple madder to make a dirty burgundy. But out in the world, I gratefully count on words to aid my clients in seeing and imagining color.

There are color names that everyone knows: school-bus yellow, cherry red, grass green. But once we work our way through the basic rainbow, we are left with millions of permutations, and this is where language becomes our handrail. Naming a color, or at least using words to describe it, allows us to communicate its essence. Words facilitate our imagination and provide the link between our eyes, voice, and mind. In fact, if a person is unable to name a color, he will have a difficult time classifying and using it. (People who experience color-grapheme synesthesia have paired sensory responses, meaning they see numbers and letters as specific colors. A person with this medical syndrome may see the letter *H* as yellow or the number 2 as blue.)

Even when we are looking at actual samples on the wall, words help to open eyes and minds. If I tell someone that I think we should try a warm, deep brown, I'll get the point across far more effectively by suggesting "dark chocolate" or "black coffee." Conversely, when I want a client to

reducing the inherent abstraction of color. I've always wanted to buy a can of their Arsenic, an intriguing turquoise-green whose name evokes the past, with a frisson of danger. Victorian ladies ingested the chemical (before it was discovered to be poisonous) in hopes of lightening their skin. Napoléon is rumored to have died from exposure to arsenic-laced wallpaper. The Farrow & Ball wall color, fortunately, is entirely nontoxic.

In this country, two masters of the art of paint naming are lifestyle gurus Martha Stewart and Ralph Lauren. Both use their paint lines to tell color-coded stories about the concepts and symbols behind their brands. Ralph tells his old-world, old-money story with aspirational names like Yacht Blue and Polo Green, while Martha uses more accessible names like Tag Sale Yellow and Garden Clog Green to convey her happy-hands-at-home world. (I got to see how Martha named her paints when I helped her develop her first paint collections. See page 149 for the details.)

See page 149 for the details.

Companies that manufacture thousands of paint colors have a particularly daunting task when it comes to naming. Benjamin Moore uses old American monikers like Quincy Tan and Valley Forge Brown for their historical colors. But once you dive into their modern palettes you'll find names such as Tangerine Dream, Tequila Lime, and Bonfire. Pratt & Lambert's names for neutrals have always resonated with me: Moth Gray, Phantom, Whale, and Olive Fog are just a few of my favorites. The Pantone company, known for its color-matching system in the printing industry, recently entered the paint world with an extensive range of colors and a separate

focus on the color itself and not on its "name," which can sometimes be distracting, I often substitute a neutral number—or a simple word like *brown*—rather than supply the often loaded name of a paint color.

Paint companies use our dependence on description to great advantage. The color chart put out by Farrow & Ball evokes a world of eccentricity and history. A British company that got its start by supplying paint to the War Office at the onset of World War II, Farrow & Ball has more recently produced the paint line for the United Kingdom's National Trust. The paint itself is of very high quality, but the color chart nomenclature is incomparable. Moreover, the historically accurate paints reference real places in Great Britain and Ireland. Names like Clunch (recalling the chalk-colored stone building blocks used in the East Anglia region of Great Britain) and Mouse's Back (in the words of Farrow & Ball's color chart, "a useful 18th c. color") build a quirky British narrative that creates a context for the firm's palette, thereby deck with scores of whites. Blanc de Blanc, Seed, Pearl Moonbeam, and Ecru are but a few of the names they have enlisted to help us make the distinctions among all the subtleties.

I can usually bring my clients around to a color with a careful choice of words. For instance, a pea green that was rejected for an entry hall got the go-ahead when I renamed it "spring green." Even when words make no direct color reference, they can influence our palette. I once suggested a pale limestone shade, Benjamin Moore's Calm, to a client. She burst out laughing. Anything with

the name Calm would never survive a single day in her busy household, she told me. And yet somehow I doubt anyone would want to name a color (or paint a room) with calm's evil twin, chaos. Lo and behold, we did paint the kitchen Calm, and though life at home remained chaotic, my client found comfort in knowing that her surroundings were technically Calm. The psychology of a color's name is powerful.

There are some names that seem to provoke an immediate trust in and allegiance to a particular color. Linen white is so universal that it appears in numerous brands as if it were a given. But the less a paint color resembles a familiar object, the more likely we are to find names that simply sound good to us without giving us any real information about what the named color might look like. Would any of us guess that Farrow & Ball's Monkey Puzzle is a dark green? A very similar color in the Fine Paints of Europe Mount Vernon Colors is named Venetian Shutter. In California Paints' Historic Colors of America, a pale sky blue is simply named Emily, while a soft lemon yellow goes by Emma. As technology provides us with even greater access to color, it will be interesting to see how we use the connotative power of language to help define our visual experiences.

White, in a Word: A Partial List for an Infinite Sea of Description

French Ivory	Paradise Beach	Parchment	Vapor Trails	Halo	Mountain Peak
White Corn	Linen	Dove Wing	Ice Cap	Ashwood	Cotton Ball
Mercury Glass	Devon Cream	Seapearl	Pale Smoke	Titanium	Alpine
Diploma	Cameo White	Gray Mist	Silver Crest	Moonshine	Lily
Silk Glove	Cookie Dough	Maritime	Paper White	Intense White	Alabaster
Macaroni	Buttermilk	Cloud	Chalk	Wisp	Cream Cloak
Snow Globe	Antique Lace	Dune	Silvery Moon	Diamond	Sea Wind
Water Glass	French Vanilla	White Down	Snowfall	Icicle	Morning Dew
Flour Sack	Seashell	Ice	Whitewash	Milkshake	Sailcloth
Wick	White Swan	Light Pewter	Tusk	White Heron	Polo Mallet
White Picket	Featherbed	Shoreline	Ballet	Whitewater	Sea Salt
Fence	Blossom	Silver Chain	Muslin	Pristine	Loft
Piano Key	Celery Salt	Horizon	Clay	Colonial Cream	Milkweed
Roman Marble	Rock Candy	Brushed	Silver Satin	Sugar Cookie	Old Map
Antler	Ancient Oak	Aluminum	Calm	Froth	Old White
Panna Cotta	Seaspray	Winterwood	Opaline	Pale Moon	Pointing
Snowy Egret	Pebble Rock	Morning Dew	Glacier	Milkyway	Strong White
Opal	Navajo White	Polar Frost	Arcadia	Chiffon	James White
Butterfield	Sandy Shore	French Canvas	Albescent	Cloud Nine	Great White
Blush	Wicker	London Fog	Overcast	Pale Powder	
Lily of the Valley	Pale Almond	Balboa Mist	Swiss Coffee	Moonlight	

2

FINDING YOUR HOME'S PALETTE

I see color all around me and collect all sorts of things as inspiration: matchbooks, scraps of paper, spools of thread, marbles, stones from everywhere, jars of earth and sand, driftwood, beach glass, shells, game pieces, dishes and glasses, hardware, notebooks, takeout menus, fabric scraps, and buttons. As much as I love using my imagination, this crazy repository of stuff helps me to brainstorm new color combinations.

The other major source of inspiration I keep on hand are my Pretty Books, binders full of photographs of houses, both inside and outside, that I have clipped from design magazines for the last ten years. A few of my friends call my Pretty Books design porn. (They *are* exciting!) I show this collection to my clients all the time. We sit in my studio and go through the books with Post-its. Inevitably, one of us will select a picture of an enormous, spectacular European castle, which on the face of it has very little to do with the farmhouse we're working on. But to dream is to be inspired. Looking at art and design books and magazines keeps my vision limber. Consider starting your own Pretty Book and filling it with images that catch your eye.

Where to Begin

Sometimes my clients hand me an object and ask me to translate it into a wall color. These treasures have included a handful of pebbles, chips of paint from actual surfaces, a favorite scarf, a green and orange brochure from a grocery store, a blue credit card, and an antique lacquered box, not to mention endless magazine clippings of houses they've admired. Simply matching the color of the

object would be easy. I could just haul the source of inspiration into the paint store and hand it over so it could be scanned with a color-matching gun. The spectrometer gun would tell the computer precisely how much and which pigments to dispense into the can, and presto—we'd have the desired color, in paint form. (For more on paint color matching, see page 215.) But having a match doesn't mean we've landed on the right color. Here's how to find it.

1 **Go on a fearless hunt for inspiring images and objects:** Search high and low through books and magazines and download images you discover online. Collect anything that has a great color or combination of colors on it, like matchbooks, postcards, takeout menus, ticket stubs, buttons, ribbon, wrapping paper, packaging—you name it. Look at fabrics, rugs, and other materials for color cues. Nothing is off-limits.

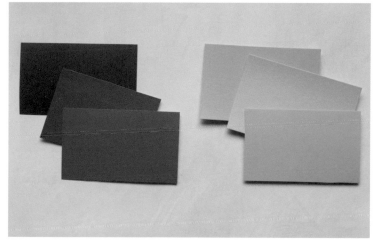

2 **Narrow down your inspiration to one or two of your favorite things** and, if possible, take your source to the paint store to select colors. If you can't bring the object with you to the store, then bring lots of paint chips back to compare them with the source. Spend time looking at the paint sample cards or chips and your inspiration. Notice how some colors jump out and some recede, how some seem murky and others quite clear. Make sure to have in hand samples that vary subtly from one another.

3 **Pick the first color that "feels" right as one of your test colors.** Then pick out two or three additional colors that depart only slightly from your favorite. Look for a chip that seems like an exact match, a lighter chip, a deeper chip, and one that looks duller or "toned down." If any of the chip colors don't appeal to you, leave them out for now. It's important to let your instincts have their say.

4 **If you are testing in an empty space, gather together fabrics, rugs, art, lamps, and anything relevant,** and arrange them near your color tests to see what works best. Like completing a puzzle, this process gets easier the closer you get to re-creating what the room will look like furnished.

5 **Select the color that you like best.** If you aren't there yet, repeat the process, further winnowing your choices through another round of color chip options.

Six Inspirations for a Palette

1 A Work of Art

One of my favorite sources of inspiration is art. Think about it: you're served up a palette on a platter because the artist has already done all the hard work of narrowing down colors and combining them in a successful composition. Here, a Giorgio Morandi painting is the jumping-off point for a room: the blue and gray vessels suggest colors for dominant surfaces like walls and ceiling, and the small sliver of orangey-red works like an accent color one might find in a vase or a throw pillow.

2 A Favorite Color

If blue's your color, run with it. I love to use variations of a color in the same room. Layering several shades of a single color—from light to dark, bright to somber—can create a visually stimulating effect. Consider all the ways in which you can introduce a color—paint, textiles, ceramics, artwork, even hardware. The swatches for my blue palette include striped rugs and several color tones to test for walls, trim, and ceiling, plus some patterned fabrics.

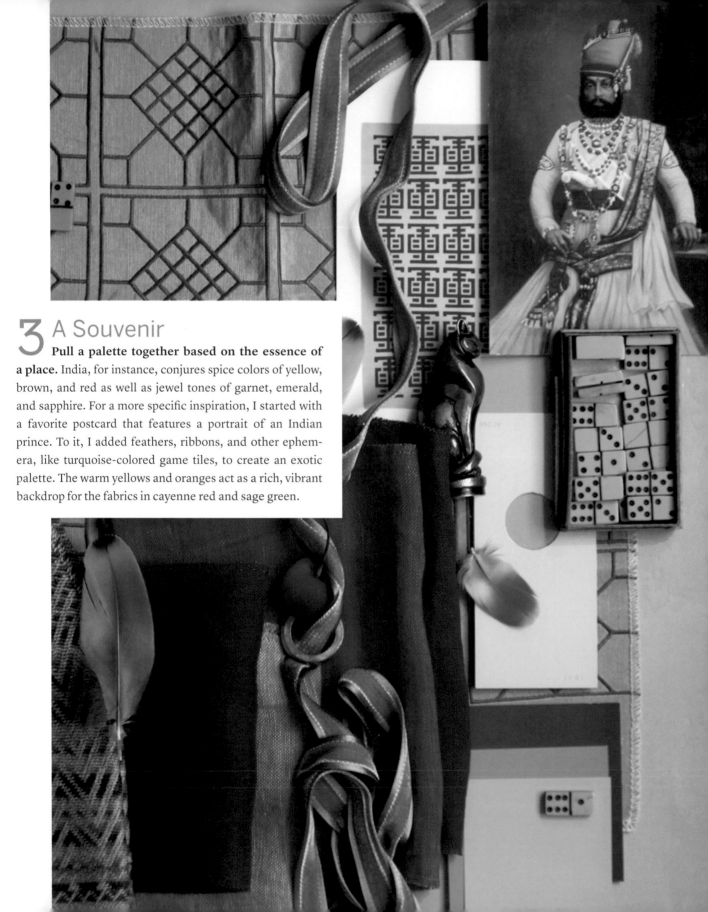

3 A Souvenir

Pull a palette together based on the essence of a place. India, for instance, conjures spice colors of yellow, brown, and red as well as jewel tones of garnet, emerald, and sapphire. For a more specific inspiration, I started with a favorite postcard that features a portrait of an Indian prince. To it, I added feathers, ribbons, and other ephemera, like turquoise-colored game tiles, to create an exotic palette. The warm yellows and oranges act as a rich, vibrant backdrop for the fabrics in cayenne red and sage green.

4 A Piece of Fabric

I love rooms that have balance and tension. One of my tricks is to take a somber, earthy, or dark palette and wake it up with an unexpected color. For a home office, I combined handsome materials like perforated stamped suede, charcoal-gray pinstripe flannel, chocolate-brown wool carpet, steel curtain rods, and deep brown textured wood cabinets with a very pale, slightly grayed lavender for the walls and a more vibrant violet for a closet interior. The cream and brown ikat fabric was chosen for curtains.

5 An Icon

Some colors and combinations are so classic, like the orange and brown Hermès box, that there's no topping them. I look to all sorts of paper goods—artfully designed packaging, stationery, posters, and wrapping paper—for color ideas. In this case, the tangerine of the banded box was the inspiration for a palette using orange, cream, gray, and brown. Putting a bold color on the wall is especially effective when you balance it with pattern, materials, and textures.

6 A Place in Time

Old houses are graced with the lovely patina of years. Draw from elegant aged materials like porcelain tubs and worn floors for subtle, neutral tones to build a quiet but stately palette. This postcard image of an old Federal-era house has been pinned on my studio bulletin board for years; I love the limestone building blocks and the tall, dark, and handsome windows. In this scheme I pulled pale grays and taupes for wall colors, extending the palette with linen upholstery fabrics and driftwood-colored floors.

From Porcelain Saucer to Paint Can

Presented with a favorite porcelain saucer by a client, this was the approach I took to translate it into a livable wall color for this traditional living room: I started with four similar paint chips from different manufacturers. I held the samples up to the dish at various angles and in different light conditions in the room. First I chose a yellow that appeared to be an "exact" match. To it, I added three other

yellows—one a bit warmer, one slightly lighter, and one that looked grayed down or "quieter." I included the quiet yellow because small doses of seemingly mild yellow can become very vibrant on a large scale. I find this to be true of many shades. Once we applied the four hues to the wall, we stood back and assessed the qualities of each sample and discussed which wall color worked best in the room.

In this case, the quiet yellow won us over. Sometimes the best color doesn't match or even evoke the source; it may be the color you least expect. That's how inspiration works: it's not about copying. It's about conjuring the right color, using a process of trial and error. The dirty yellow was a hue that escaped looking too pastel or juvenile because it was toned down and expressed some age. A yellow that was too bright would have been out of tune with the sophisticated living room. The wall color we chose, Farrow & Ball Citron, worked because it captured the *essence* of the yellow dish: unusual, fresh, refined.

3

COLOR IN CONTEXT

Every room has its own reasons for accepting or rejecting a color. Spaces are like people, each a little different from the next, and it takes time to get to know them in order to figure out what does and doesn't work. But choosing color also has as much to do with your life and your needs as with light, scale, architecture, materials, and furnishings. It's important to consider all of this as you launch into a new project. Spending a little time to learn more about your space and your preferences will help you think about color with open eyes. Over the years, I've developed approaches to various rooms and other color issues (exterior and interior) that I share here, but always with the understanding that for every idea about color, sometimes the opposite is true.

Color and Light

At the top of my list of considerations is how a room is lit—the combination of sun angles and light fixtures. Any color you choose is at that duo's mercy. Depending on where you sit on the globe, the quality and intensity of natural light will vary. And given the ebb and flow of artificial light in a room, from no lamplight to all lamplight, its palette will always be changing. I do the bulk of

my work in the New York area, but occasionally I travel to very different climates to consult on color. When I started doing jobs in Los Angeles, I had a difficult time adjusting to the glare of the sun; I was accustomed to the softer, more obstructed light of New York City. My eyes felt strained and tired quickly when looking at colors outdoors. I finally understood that in L.A. big sunglasses are a necessity, not just a fashion statement or a movie-star affectation.

Ten years ago, I taught art in the Dominican Republic. The houses in the town of La Romana were turquoise, pink, orange, and red, and everyone wore brightly colored clothing—all of which was a real sock in the eye for someone arriving in February from Manhattan. The sun was so intense and omnipresent that colors I considered bold back home grew positively pallid in the Caribbean glare. My students thought nothing of using strong, pure color straight from the can for their projects, partly out of necessity (available paint is mostly ready-made and limited at that), but mostly because they were so comfortable with bold hues. The colors suited the tropical environment, where the sun is powerful and the local temperament is relaxed. It drove home how misguided it would be to import this vibrant local palette to a northern location. There's a good reason you don't see hot-pink bungalows amid the weathered gray cottages of Nantucket.

All the vagaries of location—light, terrain, foliage, architecture—personalize our sense of color, as do materials and finishes. This section of the book will take you through them as well as the effects of windows and artificial light on the colors you choose.

Thinking About Light

1 **Color samples appear completely different under an open sky than they do indoors.** Even an overcast sky is very bright compared with interior lighting. It's always a good idea to spend time looking at how the light behaves in your particular setting, especially if you are relocating. Is it soft in the morning and glaring in the afternoon? Is it much brighter in general than your previous location? It might sound obvious, but *do not pick exterior colors while you are indoors.*

2 **Light and setting are inextricably linked.** One of my clients who had recently bought a house thought she had a pale-green guest room. She had seen the room only once or twice, on sunny summer afternoons, when we walked through the house together. I pointed out that the room was actually white—it looked green because there was a leafy maple tree right outside the window. *Pay attention to reflected light every bit as much as to direct light.*

3 **It is senseless to compete with a breath-taking view.** The living room of a rustic ranch house I worked on in southern Arizona had a spectacular corner window that looked out over the harsh but beautiful desert landscape. Rolling hills studded with grand saguaro cacti shimmered in the dry heat. In this situation it made more sense to blend with the desert by extending the sand color to the walls, which ended up being not just painted but pigmented.

4 **Know your exposures.** The way a room feels has a lot to do with how many openings it has and the temperature of the light as determined by the orientation of its windows. If the room has a southern exposure, you know how incredibly bright and warm (and damaging) the sun can be. A northern exposure is quite different, providing more neutral light that remains fairly consistent throughout the day. That's why artists' studios are traditionally oriented to the north. Eastern and western exposures are the morning and afternoon timekeepers. The same red installed in rooms oriented to each of the cardinal points would appear to be four distinct colors, with even more permutations depending on the time of day. The sun is a decision-maker.

5 **Don't forget the surfaces.** Surface quality affects how light interacts with color. Glossy surfaces reflect light and obscure color, making a space more visually stimulating. Dull surfaces absorb light, often making colors appear denser and rooms calmer. Pay attention to the many ways surfaces react to light and to one another, and don't forget to factor in a paint's level of sheen when selecting a color.

Day and Night

Light affects everything—our moods, our minds, and our homes. This simple but elegant house shows us just how much natural light affects the exterior color palette, even in a short span of time. The pale cedar shingles shift from light beige in the late afternoon to cool gray in the early evening. The dark voids of the daytime windows turn to yellow and blue as night falls. (The blue emanating from the upstairs bedroom comes from a light sculpture located near the window.) Try photographing your own house at different times of the day and early evening. You'll discover where shadows fall, which aspect of the house is sunlit the longest, and which sits in shade most of the day. This information is helpful when you begin considering exterior colors and critical when it comes to making a final selection, so be sure to test your color on more than one exterior wall.

About Windows

Sunrooms, Two Ways

People often think that a sunroom doesn't need color since wraparound windows dominate the space, but the color of those window frames can change the feel of the room dramatically. I've found that black window frames allow our eyes to travel to the outside more easily than white frames do. I'm always asked if black will confine, shrink, or overpower a room. For many people the very idea of black window frames runs counter to everything they think of when it comes to a sunroom. But, in fact, dark frames are great for bright rooms because they recede and demand little attention from our eyes as we take in the room and the view.

Of course, there's nothing wrong with painting your window frames white or a light color either. The effect is very different and sometimes quite desirable. White-windowed sunrooms feel and look fresh and bright. Light window frames actually slow your eye way down and keep your focus on the things in the room longer. This might be just the trick if your view is less than perfect. And even if your view is spectacular, sometimes it's nice to feel the boundaries of a beautiful room, especially if it's cold outside.

Considering Contrast

There's a big difference between sunrooms (rooms that are almost all windows) and sunny rooms (rooms, particularly south-facing, that get a lot of sunlight through just a few openings). Rooms with few windows that get intense amounts of sun can be challenging to live in if you paint them deep colors. A deep wall color will greatly increase the contrast between the windows and the walls, causing your eyes to work overtime as they adjust to the dynamic shift between light and dark. Many of us find the eyestrain distracting and will want to avoid creating this condition, but some people love this effect. In bedrooms, mostly nighttime spaces, dark walls can contribute to creating an alluring retreat.

Window Treatments

Especially in rooms with lots of light, paint color choices must go hand in hand with decisions about window treatments. Modulating the light can range from simply filtering it with screenlike solar shades to completely blocking it out with heavy curtains or blackout shades. Keep in mind that the material of the window treatments itself, its color and translucency, will affect room colors. Consider nighttime conditions too, particularly if you have picture windows or large expanses of glass. There's nothing more unsettling than feeling exposed or onstage when darkness falls. Blinds or curtains will "protect" you as well as avoid the "big black slab" effect of large windows at night.

Artificial Light

People who visit my city apartment always remark on how welcoming it is. Few realize how many artificial light sources are at work to make the environment so "naturally" warm. In my living room, a space that measures thirteen by eighteen feet, six different light sources are all key players: a reading lamp by the sofa, a pair of lamps on the bookcase, a hidden uplight atop a tall cabinet, a big Noguchi paper floor lamp, and last but not least, my TV, an element often overlooked as a light, even though we all recognize the cool flicker when we see it through windows at night. A "successful" room needs a minimum of three artificial light sources that include different kinds of fixtures, with as many dimmers as possible. Look at rooms you love and count the light sources; a great room has a lot.

I've never worked on an interior that didn't have artificial light sources affecting my perception of color. All sources of light have color temperatures. We often refer to light as warm or cool, with most of us preferring warmer light sources for residential spaces. Man-made light can actually change the color you see on your walls considerably. Make sure that you look at your sample paint colors in the kind of light that will inhabit the space once your project is finished. It's painful to think of spending a lot of time and energy selecting the perfect color, only to have it remixed by a simple lightbulb.

Lightbulbs

When choosing lightbulbs, consider the color of the light they emit. The most common types are the following:

1 **Tungsten incandescent.** The most familiar, and a direct descendant of the bulb patented by Edison in 1879, it produces a light much warmer than even the sun. Most of us find it flattering and easy on the eyes. Unfortunately its beautiful light is also inefficient so it is rapidly being replaced by CFLs.

2 **Compact fluorescent (CFL).** Lasting up to fifteen times longer than the average incandescent bulb (and consequently Energy Star–rated by the U.S. and Canadian governments), this bulb increasingly rules the hardware store shelves. Although manufacturers are racing to make CFLs as appealing as incandescents, which are being phased out, we're not there yet. The quality of light they produce is still unpopular because people see it as "flat," "blue," and "cold." Moreover, there are concerns that fluorescent lighting is harmful to artwork, causing works on paper to fade irreparably.

3 **Halogen.** A variation of incandescent technology (it also uses a tungsten filament, combined with halogen gas), these bulbs produce the "whitest" light of any bulb. They are typically more expensive than other types but are capable of producing up to 30 percent more light. Excellent for general lighting and, because of their clean, clear light, especially well suited to task lighting and for bathrooms.

Day and Night

My friend Gil Schafer's dining room is a reading room by day, with beautiful books stacked in piles all around a big table anchored by two tall lamps. Come evening, if he's entertaining, he clears away the books, dims the lamps, and sprinkles votive candles across the table. The walls in his dining room are persimmon, an orangey-red that's friendly by day, elegant at night, and a warm complement to his many antiques all the time. It's a room you always want to be in.

Exterior Colors

Most of us live near other people and buildings, whether in a small town, a suburb, or a bustling city. I grew up in a village of small, mostly white 1920s houses, shaded by big trees. For our house, my mother chose a medium gray for the body and a deep yellow ochre for the shutters and trim. It wasn't especially wild, but it stood out, which was, I think, my mother's goal. Bland things bored her, and she couldn't have cared less about relating to the colors of the neighbors' houses. Most of us, though, try to be sensitive to neighboring architecture when choosing exterior colors.

When I work on an exterior project, I consider the architectural style and size of the building and the materials used to construct it, as well as the light angles, the proximity of neighboring buildings, the tone of the area, and my client's temperament and goals. Sometimes I'll take my client for a drive and we'll talk about which houses we like and why. You may even get lucky and stumble upon the perfect palette.

If you buy a house in a historic district, note that these zones often have strict rules regarding exterior paint as well as window and door style, materials, even house numbers. The goal is to create and maintain a cohesive visual environment respectful of the past. Start by walking around your neighborhood, taking note of the colors and combinations you like, since the palette of nearby houses no doubt satisfies whatever local restrictions may exist. It pays to look into these. I once received an urgent plea for help when the grout on a client's freshly repointed brick town house was deemed "too bright" by the inspector from the Landmarks Department. I ended up making a stain that workers painstakingly applied to all the grout so that my client could obtain permits to continue his restoration.

Newer suburbs have their own brand of uniformity, with nearly identical houses made even more anonymous by a sameness of palette, due to the use of materials like asphalt roofing shingles and vinyl siding and windows that offer limited choices of color. You may have few options regarding what you can paint, especially if you don't want to compromise the low-maintenance convenience of materials like vinyl. Still, a door with a distinctive color is an easy identifier. ("My house is the one with the shiny green door.") Aside from painting, you can always highlight your house with planters brimming with bright flowers.

In a row of identical nineteenth-century houses with uniform white trim, a variety of clapboard colors in equally soft tones adds life to the street and allows each home to remain distinct. A brick sidewalk ties the houses together.

The defined areas of this mid-century house's façade provide a perfect canvas for bold blocks of color. Few houses present this opportunity, so it's great to see someone take full advantage of color on modern architecture and push past the tyranny of white.

Surface Materials

Many of my clients ask me to use color to "fix" a material that, while functional, would not normally suit their aesthetic. Even in major renovations, it's not uncommon to try to work around such expensive elements as granite countertops and marble floors. I find that almost all materials will yield color suggestions. When they don't, there are still ways to make them work. Even homely bathroom tiles can be painted over. When you create a new color context, an element you may at first have rejected can take on a whole new character.

Painting over things like brick and bare wood might seem heretical but in fact could be the best decision you can make for a space. Yes, natural wood can be spectacular and fine woodwork exquisite, but not all of it is special. I will paint just about anything if I think doing so will make it look better. I am always surprised by the number of people who labor to remove acres of paint from moldings and doors in older homes. Ironically, most of these architectural elements of common woods were originally designed to be painted; their mismatched grains and colors were never meant to be exposed.

When it comes to interior brick walls, I usually cover them with several coats of paint. I know there's an exposed-brick fan club; I'm just not a member. The color of brick presents challenges to many styles of decorating, as does its texture and pattern. A coat of paint can calm the noise. In my studio in a 150-year-old industrial loft space in SoHo, it was the only way to unite the hodgepodge of materials—patterned pressed tin, rough-hewn wood, plywood, brick, Sheetrock, exposed pipes, and two types of window frames. A total whitewash created a neutral backdrop for the color work I do.

It's impressive what a few cans of white paint can accomplish, totally transforming what was once a small barn. Imagine how gloomy it would be without its coat of whitewash. Now three small windows are enough to light the room. The white quiets the exposed structure of the room while the unpainted ceiling drops a "lid" on the space.

This kitchen tucks into the lower level of an old New York town house. This room could be foreboding in its original brick state, but white paint rescues it, helping light infiltrate, reflect, and brighten. The white also allows the staircase, which leads up to the backyard and the rest of the house, to take on, in its coat of dark gray, a more sculptural quality.

Color and Elements of a Room

The way a room is constructed will affect how you want to use color. Traditional architecture has moldings that frame walls and openings. This makes it easy to start and stop a wall or ceiling color. Traditional architecture also typically has more doors that lead to hallways, closets, bathrooms, or other areas. Rooms with a lot of windows and doors can often hold a powerful color well because

when the walls are broken up by openings, so too is the color.

Interiors with plenty of trim present a choice—to highlight it or not to. The classic preference in trim color, especially for pale-colored rooms, has been white or off-white. Bright whites are more modern, while softer, toned, or "off" whites are well-suited for more classic or historical rooms. This tone-on-tone or mostly white or light scheme creates a quieter, more seamless shell for a room's furnishings. Adding some drama while still maintaining a degree of calm can be achieved by painting the moldings and walls of a room a single, weightier color like a warm taupe in different finishes: flat for walls, glossier for trim.

Painting moldings a contrasting color to that of the walls produces the effect of a line drawing its way around the room. The higher the contrast, the more the molding acts as a frame setting apart sections of walls and views from room to room. Painting any detail a strong color will draw attention to it, thus changing the room's focal points and sense of scale. Even something simple like painting the doors to other rooms or closets a unique color will change the way you perceive space. The most challenging paint schemes pair

colorful walls with colorful trim. Venturing into this territory isn't easy, but it can be really fun, interesting, and beautiful. You'd be surprised what combinations a little trial and error can produce.

The simplicity of contemporary architecture with its flowing spaces and absence of trim would seem to alleviate color quandaries by reducing the number of choices that need to be made. But in fact color decisions become more critical. The very pared-down nature of such architecture poses a lot of difficulties in starting or stopping colors. The lack of molding around doors can make it next to impossible to achieve a delicate color transition from one room to the next. Large uninterrupted walls can feel overpowering when painted a "big" color. The size of a room can help determine how it will hold color. Large rooms often need lighter colors so they don't become overpowering. And a smaller room, like a dining room, can benefit from a deeper color to support the intimacy of sharing a meal. Since living rooms and dining rooms are frequently connected, this color relationship can be made subtle or more dramatic, depending on your goals. With any room, time spent assessing your environment is never wasted; understanding your space will help guide you to the right colors for it.

Ceilings

There is no rule that says ceilings have to be white, though it is often the appropriate choice. If I've put a distinct color on the walls and want them to be the focal point, I'll keep the ceiling light. In bathrooms, where you want to see yourself in the cleanest, clearest light, a white or light ceiling color is probably best, though a touch of pink can cast a flattering glow. Putting color on the ceilings is one more thing to figure out, but it can be worth the extra effort. Because it's unexpected, it's a pick-me-up, psychologically and visually. I've done kids' rooms with white walls and a bright ceiling color—a top to a toy box, if you will. For a master bedroom with hand-painted French wallpaper, I chose a delicate celadon green, just a wisp of color.

Because they are rarely directly illuminated by natural light, ceilings respond to any kind of light far differently than walls. Unusually high ceilings often "disappear" above light fixtures, especially at night. If you have recessed ceiling fixtures, then your ceiling will sit in the dark when your lights are on. Fixtures that throw light up onto the ceiling will obviously highlight any color you apply. Very low ceilings can be oppressive and require a color that doesn't add weight.

A deep sky color sits like a lid atop modern white walls. The ceiling color takes its cue from, and expands upon, the large domed light fixture above the dining table.

In this traditional room with creamy white walls, the decorative painted ceiling creates a strong visual impact. Clearly the Oriental rug was the inspiration for the multi-toned ceiling, which casts a diffuse reflection of the rug back into the room.

Floors

Few people look at the floor when choosing a room's color. But they should, as it has a big impact on a room's palette. Floors can be beautiful elements in any space or distractions that demand too much attention. Obviously, the more open space you have, the more apparent the floor will be. Lofts are often very "floory." It helps to consider how much flooring material you will see or want to see when planning your room. Large rugs absorb light that would otherwise scatter across a hard-surface floor. The most important thing to know is that floors can influence color every bit as much as walls and ceilings.

Have you ever noticed how the blackest of floors doesn't seem dark at all when light hits it? Any shiny surface will reflect light, regardless of its color, so keep that in mind when you consider floor finishes and sealers. Light bouncing off hard-surface floors can also reflect some of the floor color onto the walls. And a color used on the floor will look much lighter than it does on the wall.

My clients ask me all the time about staining wood floors. I prefer a dark brown stain like a walnut for a floor because it is neutral when combined with other colors. A cherry or mahogany stain can give a red cast that will compete with many wall colors, and a maple stain or varnished oak floors can look very yellow.

This client wished to replicate the rustic look of old floors she had seen and loved in Sweden. For her living room's pine herringbone floors, I created a pale gray stain to achieve the desired effect. The floors, along with the antique mantelpiece, give the modern white room a sense of history.

Patterned tiles create a permanent "rug" in this entrance hall, while the painted wood floor in the background reflects ambient light and the photo collection.

A glossy black is never as dark as you think it will be. In this kitchen, the floor acts like a tranquil reflecting pool, effectively doubling the size of the window.

49

Trim

Let's face it, wall color dominates our palette decisions. The very thought of finding a color for trim as well can overwhelm us right back to white. Trim shows up in many guises, depending on the age and style of a house. It can be opulent, lacy, ornamental, and abundant. Or it may be minimal, underwhelming, and not worth noticing. And then there are the countless versions of trim in between. Your trim may be something that you want to hide or highlight once you've considered the overall space you're painting.

Our eyes race to details, edges where colors meet, and contrasting textures, so if your trim is not worthy, or simply not your style, make it recede by using a similar color for everything. A surefire way to make it practically disappear is to cloak it in the same color as the walls. This is a great way to modernize an older, ornately trimmed room. You can even use the same sheen on both walls and trim, such as eggshell, which has a dull, washable finish. This helps to embed the trim in one even coat, leaving only shadows to reveal it.

Hiding trim is not just a technique to use on over-the-top bygone-era molding that's thwarting your mid-century design scheme. Underscaled, uneventful trim often doesn't do well when highlighted or contrasted with the walls. Hide it. The same goes for old door frames, window moldings, and baseboards whose fine lines and profiles disappeared long ago under layers of paint. Add yet another in a color that matches your walls so the uneven edges disappear.

Of course, some houses present scads of opportunities to highlight trim. If you are lucky enough to have a house with great proportions and lovely moldings, you may want to go the extra mile and select colors that coordinate with your walls and furnishings to highlight the architecture. Contrasting colors for walls and trim create distinct boundaries. White trim in a dark room will be bold and act as a framing device, as will dark trim in a white room. A more subtle relationship between wall and trim is to start with a light wall color and move several degrees deeper for the trim, or work in reverse and pair lighter trim with deeper walls in the same color family.

Walls of books bring color, texture, detail, interest, and density to a room. Bookcases and the trim around them can be an excellent place to use bolder color or add detail to moldings. I love the two tones of cool gray used on the shelves and door in this library. It's the perfect setup for the rich red inside the shelves.

On close inspection you'll see that this quiet gray room has no end of trim: tall baseboards, picture frame molding, picture rail molding, and crown molding. Painting everything from the floor to the crown molding all one color smoothes out the room, letting only shadow indicate the presence of trim detail.

Furnishings

If you are working with existing furnishings, then you already have many pieces of your color puzzle. If you are starting from scratch, you can approach your room in one of two ways. Either start by selecting colors for your room and then go about finding furnishings, or find a couple of big things, like a rug or a sofa, and derive your paint colors from them. The color-first approach gives you a starting point, which can be really helpful for some people. The stuff-first, color-second approach means that you can find something you love without worrying about whether it will work with the walls.

For example, build a palette around colors in the fabric of your favorite chair. I work with textiles all the time. Many of my clients paint and repaint before they reupholster their furniture (something you may want to consider before you commit to a "green today, gone tomorrow" pattern for your sofa). The colors in a fabric may lead you to a harmonious or a contrasting palette, but either way, the fabric will help to narrow your path. Or you may find inspiration in something else at home, like a collection. Photographs, pottery, shells—just about anything can be a great first step in building a color palette.

One Fabric, Three Palettes

Take a fabric sample from, say, your living room sofa as the foundation for building a color scheme. Want a tranquil room? Stick close to the light tones in the fabric; go with a pale stone color. Too quiet? Pump up the color by pulling a hue from the brightest stripe, but go a few shades lighter in its color family (here, a soft lavender). Ready to be daring? Try a shade as bold as the most colorful stripe in the fabric (purple) but in an altogether different color (in this case, green).

The large stenciled border around the top of this bedroom is not an exact replica of the bedcover, but it works beautifully as a close reference. Together the border and the bedspread provide a nice top and bottom framing of the powder-blue walls. Fabrics are a great source of both color and pattern inspiration.

53

Art

Color invites color to the party. Except, it seems, when it comes to color behind art. Scores of architects, art dealers, and curators are poised to issue subpoenas for this dreadful offense, but just because they're authoritative doesn't mean they're right. A rich terra-cotta, for instance, can elevate a group of black-and-white photographs from random to curated. A band of blue that picks up the color in a set of prints can be the thread that pulls them all together.

The British artist Howard Hodgkin, known for his masterful and free use of color, and a favorite of mine, spends a great deal of time carefully orchestrating the wall colors and finishes of spaces where his work will be exhibited. For his retrospective at the Tate in London, he chose dark gray, buttermilk, and coffee colors, applied with loose, visible brush marks. Though critics balked, Hodgkin insists that these tonal hues prevent his smallish paintings from being overwhelmed by unmitigated white walls.

The robin's-egg blue of the frames for these black-and-white engravings relates to the pale sage blue of the wall behind, yet still sets the collection apart. Colorless art presents endless options for wall and frame colors. This palette is just colorful enough to create a distinct feeling for the room and just quiet enough not to overwhelm the delicate aspects of the engravings.

One Painting, Four Backgrounds

The color behind artwork alters the way we see it in a space. This photograph takes on different qualities depending on the color it's displayed on. White causes it to hover yet still connects to the borders of the postcards. Green makes the orange and red, its complement, vibrate with energy. Gray quiets the image while still providing contrast. The sand color connects to the lower portion of the photograph and embeds the picture in the surrounding wall color.

Using Color to Define Space

I believe that you can use any color anywhere, so long as you use the right dose. In my living room I have a band of grayish purple that runs along one wall and acts as a visual parking space for a burnt-orange mid-century cabinet. To my eye, the purple is as big as it can be without overstepping its bounds. I wanted an unusual and bold color statement in this room, but the particulars of

the space—the light, architectural details, and dimensions—did not support coating it entirely in color. Color proportion can be a really fun thing to experiment with, in bands, blocks, stripes, even as small accents. Vibrant yellow, for instance, can bring a room to life when applied to a door or a table; blanket the walls in the same color, however, and you risk sending the room (and its occupants) over the edge. I recently painted just the narrow door frames to my kitchen yellow. It was an experiment, to add a bright accent to a room that is otherwise predominantly sober grays and blacks. I like it; it's jaunty. But who knows how long the yellow note will last. I'm always playing with color.

Color can be used to define volume; shift our focus, giving us a visual destination; and even give a room a whole new character. As a color consultant I am often left with the task of "fixing" quirky, odd, and difficult interior spaces to make them easier on the eye and more user-friendly. Color can be used to adjust our sense of space. In a large, awkwardly shaped room, I'll sometimes paint a wall or part of a wall a different color to create a focal point. This attracts the eye, giving it a place to look first before taking in the rest of the

space. If you want to enhance a particular wall, aside from painting it a separate color you can cover it with a material like wood, stone, or paper. Like a work of art, a highlighted wall becomes an element in its own right, and an expression of imagination.

Color can also work as camouflage. Running a single color up a wall and across an oddly angled ceiling can integrate the planes in a continuous field of color. To further emphasize the volume of a room or an object, "dip" it in a single color. A room dipped in white or a room dipped in, say, deep plum is equally transporting—one sends you out, the other pulls you in. Both these approaches work especially well with contemporary architecture, due to the general absence of trim and embellishment. But even traditional, heavily detailed interior spaces can be modernized and transformed when all surfaces are painted just one color. Color can also visually alter the proportions of a room, change the size you perceive a space to be, or simply shift its atmosphere. A small white room may seem dreary despite the conventional wisdom that says small spaces must be light. Paint that same small space cocoa brown and it radiates appeal, becoming the coziest nest ever.

Sight Lines

Many houses and apartments have a central room that is like the hub of a wheel. And from the hub you can see one, two, or maybe several rooms. These rooms can be hard to pick colors for, since they are in constant communication with their neighbors. Sometimes adjacent colors get along splendidly—mocha with cream, violet with ochre. At other times, there is no color harmony, often because the relationship among connected rooms wasn't taken into consideration.

There are various ways to approach a room-to-room color scheme. You can opt for subtle color shifts or go with something dramatic and transporting. I've worked on projects where we've done bright, open living rooms next to dark, cozy libraries. Just a glimpse of a strong color can pique curiosity and generate movement. I once put a deep red room at the end of a long white hallway whose walls were hung with framed black-and-white photographs. The red room created a theatrical and evocative destination. I've also worked on palettes for several New York apartments where all the rooms were painted light colors, allowing them to flow together seamlessly. A quieter palette makes the most of limited space. The more hues and objects in a space, the more your eyes dart around, searching for a place to land. A quiet color scheme in a sparsely decorated room is restful and allows the eye to slow down.

Painting a hallway black makes the most of an already tunnel-like space, playing up the contrast between narrow passageway and tall open space at the end. The long, narrow light above a collection of pictures reinforces the horizontal feel of the hallway while also tempering and punctuating the darkness.

Gray-washed floors unite three spaces—living room, hall, dining room—that stack visually. The lime green of the far room creates a destination. Natural wood trim provides color in the white room, while white trim frames the colorful rooms.

From a chartreuse hallway, a doorway filled with pink provokes curiosity. Opposites by nature, these two colors are related in value and a classic combination in decorating.

Create a More Intimate Space

For an especially tall or narrow room, try one of my favorite tricks: bring the ceiling down to a more comfortable height by picking your ideal ceiling height and painting your wall color up to that point. This works best when there's a contrast between wall and ceiling. The wall color becomes a band around the room, leaving the upper region as a floating lid. By dividing the top and bottom, you simply and dramatically rescale the room.

Confine Bold Color

In love with a color that would blow you away if you painted the whole room with it? Try tucking it into cabinets, closets, powder rooms, or bookcases. Bold colors can go anywhere in the right dose. The coral interior of this cupboard provides a lively and amazing showcase for a collection of old blue-and-white china. Close the doors and the surprise remains hidden, allowing you to live with a big color in small doses.

Balance a Strong Color

Two ways to mitigate the impact of strong color in a room are to hang lots of art or to add bookcases to break up the expanse. Both methods keep the color from overwhelming the room. In this corridor, a series of paintings accomplishes three things. It breaks up the solid expanse of black wall above the wainscoting; it establishes a rhythm that continues right on around the corner; and it ties together the white and black of the hallway.

Changing Scale with Color

Longing for architecture that doesn't exist? Try using paint to create and shape space. Enormous tortoise shells hang on columns created with nothing but paint. The wide white bands of color bracket the fireplace, providing a perfect display for the shells and changing the focus of the room. Strong verticals make the ceiling seem higher and draw the eye upward. Our sense of space in this room would be very different if the columns disappeared.

Composing with Black

If you balk at the idea of using black as a color inside, you are not alone; many people have a fear of the dark. But black, as well as colors in the almost-black family like the deepest tones of midnight blue, charcoal gray, and aubergine, can be used with great success in shaping, organizing, and even extending space. A dark floor will anchor a room. If it's glossy it will reflect light and actually brighten the space. Black doors and trim create a handsome framing device, ironically working the same way white does to neutrally contain a wall color. Black bookcases and open shelving have a wonderful way of absorbing clutter and creating a kind of contained order. I love the way black furniture punctuates light rooms like sculpture in a museum. Blackboard paint is not only resilient but also works as a luscious matte surface—and not just in kids' rooms. I recently applied it to the lower half of my kitchen walls; its depth and deep tone work beautifully as a backdrop for bottles, utensils, containers, and nicely designed small appliances. Dramatic yet solid, black has a place in many rooms.

In a narrow hall, a glossy black floor, like a deep pool of water, visually doubles the space. Though the floor color is dark, the finish allows the white walls to be reflected, turning the hall into a slice of space with real depth.

In what is technically an open kitchen, appliances, counter, and open shelves are neatly contained in a chic black box. The rectangle of black is a strong form echoing that of the dining table, all set off by a shell of pure white.

White on Purpose

White has kept me in business for years. I rarely work on a project that doesn't involve white paint. White has seemingly endless permutations. We have countless cultural associations attached to white—restraint, purity, cleanliness, sophistication. Many of the interiors I've worked on have been exclusively white. You would think that would simplify my job, but creating a monochromatic palette is a brainteaser because working within a narrow spectrum requires nuance. I had a lovely client, a film producer, who lived in a big loft space. She spent lots of time around creative people and loved color, but only on small objects. Her Japanese mother was a master at origami, and we talked about how creased paper catches light. During our first meeting I folded a piece of white paper so that it had many facets, each reflecting the light differently. We developed a plan to paint her loft using eight different whites—the folded paper writ large. The result was subtle and conceptual, with the various whites pushing walls deeper into shadow or pulling them forward into light. There was nothing unintentional or indecisive about the whites selected for this space.

Ironically, the prevalence of white in Western architecture has its roots in the mistaken belief that the ancient Greeks lived in a pristine and formal world of bleached marble. Even after it was discovered that Athens looked a lot more like Las Vegas than like a bright white architectural model, countless minds could not be swayed.

White can reflect more personality than one would imagine. It's a seemingly simple color that often provokes a complex response. While some might find cool white sterile, others find it restful and refreshing. Like a glass of spring water, its austerity is clarifying, its "cleanliness" purifying. Others take comfort in warm whites, off-whites, and old whites, which, like bleached bones, seem to reach across time and out to nature. Cool white embraces the machine; warm white the organic.

White works wonders for many rooms, buildings, and things. It's very effective at brightening a dark space and unifying disparate elements. It can create a sense of spaciousness. The only problem with white is that it is the one color not so much chosen as defaulted to. White can be considered inoffensive and nondescript—too often the color of indecision, as opposed to the considered choice. Most of the people I know who live in white boxes do so either because they found them that way, or out of habit or trepidation. More than 80 percent of the paint that leaves the store with overwhelmed shoppers is some version of white.

When looking for the right white for your project, search for clues in fabrics, art, and objects in your room. Even small details like tile grout can help you find the right white. When I was renovating my apartment bathroom, I had a hard time selecting a wall color because I was fixated on the creamy hue of the subway tile. Nothing worked until I started looking at slightly deeper whites—colors that were closer to the grout. Having the wall hue connect to the grout color allowed the tiles to float in the space, producing a subtle but beautiful effect.

Old White

In an older building, we expect a softer effect from white. I like to select whites that look as if they've long belonged in the house. Warmer, toned-down whites, like worn wood flooring and stone sills, and even old prints, express some age and character. An overly clean, bright white will often read as out of place and glaring in an older house, especially if you are working with more classical decoration. For the same reason, if you're going for a more eclectic look, mixing old and new, then a bright white may provide a dramatic juxtaposition to the historical architecture.

New White

When dealing with modern interiors, I often go with a clean, clear white that doesn't "tip" in any discernible color direction, like warm yellow or cool blue, and doesn't look old or dirty. A "pure" white is not only devoid of other colors but is also free of associations. We think of white as colorless. To find a true white, try holding your color chips up to a piece of plain white copy paper. All whites will look warmer or deeper than the paper, but this will help you see which color chips are closest to pure white.

Breaking the Color Rules

We've all heard the color dictates, those rules, pronounced by architects, designers, decorators, and shelter magazines, that tell us what we can and cannot do. "Dark colors make a room look smaller," they warn us. Or, "White makes a room look larger." In some cases they are right—but not always. I break color rules all the time because, in my experience, a rule is only a guideline to

support what you already want to do, to dismiss, or to tweak as you see fit. Here are ten color dictums that I've come across again and again and that I think are worth rethinking. Just remember that, as with all generalities, it's the exceptions that often prove most interesting. So loosen up, be irreverent, and trust your instincts.

1 "Pink Is for Girls"

Some of my favorite rooms break this rule with abandon. Decades ago, the famous British decorator John Fowler used a shade akin to the pressed powder that you see in vintage compacts (now known as Fowler Pink), applying it to living rooms, libraries, and even bedrooms not designated for the ladies. A soft pale pink is beautiful in almost any room, casting a glow that makes everyone in it look the picture of health— but do note that this shade needs to be anchored. Offset its sweetness with handsome dark woods, upholstery in deep tones, and "masculine" metals like iron and bronze. The decidedly pink hotel room opposite is a splendid example of breaking this rule with impunity. The simple painted brown line that borders the top of the walls, the regal blue velvet upholstery, and the bold metal nail heads all work in concert to temper the opinionated pink, creating a gender-neutral balance.

2 "Brown Is for Boys"

Many of my clients worry that brown is too masculine to use just anywhere. Not so, I say. Perhaps if it's cohabitating with leather, iron, and stone, but what if it's buttered up with pale warm colors or sent on a hot date with bright pink, rich red, or lavender? Or even balanced with nothing but white? A rich chocolate brown makes a distinct and universally appealing backdrop to the suite of white decorative elements here. We assign meaning, gender, and emotions to colors, but context is everything, so it's safe to say that the pairing of colors with opposite associations will balance out the baggage to a great degree.

3 "Never Use One Color for Everything"

Traditional architecture is filled to the rafters with trim—door frames, baseboards, chair rails, picture moldings, window casements, and crown moldings. And tradition says these elements should be one color, usually white, while the walls are painted a contrasting color. This rule has become almost a given, so much so that we don't even think of painting the trim anything but white. I do it too, because it works beautifully in many homes. White creates a clean, distinct, and unifying border that connects spaces. But this is another way I sometimes break the rules. Painting the trim the same color as the walls is a powerful way to simplify and modernize older styles of architecture. By using one color, or even two that are very close in value, you reduce the visual stimulation and eliminate the graphic, linear quality created by contrasting trim. Your eye takes in the whole room rather than settling on a detail. I've seen Victorian houses blanketed in a single color to spectacular effect. The result is simultaneously dramatic and calming.

4 "Stay Away from Black"

Breaking this rule is like skipping class for the first time. It feels liberating and dangerous all at once. I realize that black is firmly off-limits for most people, but I've come to believe in black magic. In my mind, black is the new white for trim. I love black windows frames, baseboards, door frames—you name it. Black is handsome and substantive, lending gravitas to a pale hue or grounding whimsy. It is also great at defining an area like a niche, providing focus in a large space, or changing a room's scale. Cutting loose with a freehand application of black in a white room can transform it utterly from a plain box to a charcoal drawing you step into. As in fashion, black is authoritative and daring, but in interiors, it's also refreshing.

5 "Bathrooms Should Be Light"

It makes sense that most people paint their bathrooms white or a light color. You want to be able to clearly see what you're doing, and it's important for the room to feel fresh and clean. But bathrooms are filled with reflective materials that, by bouncing light around, help to illuminate the space, which can present an opportunity to expand the palette. Darker colors work as a counterpoint to porcelain and mirrors. A deeper hue for a bathroom—midnight blue or charcoal gray—can transform a clinical space into a comfortable room to be enjoyed at one's leisure. Powder rooms, because they tend to be small and infrequently used, also present an opportunity to use a varied palette (see page 118). Windowless spaces especially rely on wall color, whether in paint or patterned wallpaper, to lend the room some personality. This room should be an unexpected treat, so go for broke.

6 "Dark Colors Are Too Difficult"

Why are we comfortable painting a study a dark color but balk at the notion of casting a dining room in a more mysterious light? Deep colors create moods. They can be soothing, romantic, evocative, and grounding. After a long day in a brightly lit, glaring workspace, returning home to the embrace of a deeply hued room can be transformative. Dark colors can also rescue rooms like kitchens from the gloom brought on by the one-two punch of dull fluorescent lighting hitting dull laminate surfaces. Rich colors draw the eye away from mundane materials. So don't rule out deep colors because you are afraid of the dark.

7 "Color Can't Travel"

It's really hard not to be wildly inspired by colors in faraway places; in fact, it's one of the things that makes travel so compelling. Who hasn't dreamed of bringing home a color as a favorite souvenir? I've done it: gone to an island, lost myself to the light and the sea, and thought, "That color is perfect for my bedroom." Long story short—yikes, what was I thinking? My bedroom gets muted northern light—it just can't handle turquoise. If there is a rule about vacation colors, it should be that if you're going to live with them as happily back home as on holiday, they are going to have to undergo an alteration in intensity, material, or size. This is especially true of vibrant hues experienced in brilliant sunshine. Be inspired by the colors you see on your journeys but don't be literal (for advice on translating inspiration into wall colors, see page 20). Take those indelible color memories and translate them into softer patches of wall color (in a niche, framing a painting) or into usable accents, like a bowl for your table or a throw for your bed. This is the one time when a single element, not a whole room, may be more evocative and pleasing.

8 "Old Houses Get Historic Colors"

Not all old houses come with time-stamped labels like Colonial, craftsman, Victorian, or modern, but many do. And for the owners of those examples of specific period building styles, color choices can feel predetermined. Does a Victorian house have to be painted in a Victorian color palette? Does a modern house have to be all white? If you live in a historic district, you might be limited in the colors you can use on the exterior of your home. On the other hand, you may be able to cut loose like the Boston homeowners whose red shingle and school-bus yellow stucco house (left) flies in the face of its sedate redbrick neighbors on Beacon Hill.

The truth is that many historically accurate palettes would feel dreary, drab, dark, or oppressive to us now. Not only do we have and expect more interior light, but we also have access to brighter colors as well as multiple shades of a single hue. On the interior, color is up to you, so feel free to follow your impulses. I love to mix historical colors with more lively hues to update a house or a room.

9 "Art Belongs on White Walls"

I love seeing color behind art, though it's not often you find it. Most galleries hang art on white walls, and collectors follow suit, as do most mere mortals. We fear that a color on the walls will be too decorative and disrespectful of the art. But what's at stake here is the art; will it be enhanced or diminished by being viewed against a field of color? In an entry foyer, a soft gray is the perfect foil for an intimate color photograph framed in white that would be lost on a white wall (right). Similarly, old portraits with deep black backgrounds spring to life against a field of modern lime green (below).

10 "When in Doubt, Play It Safe"

If ever there was a rule to break, it's this one.
A neutral palette can be a real clunker in poorly lit spaces or rooms that have no interesting features. I don't avoid neutrals, but I do try to sort out the dull hues from the livelier ones (a process of trial and error that has everything to do with your lighting conditions). If you are new to taking risks with color, spend time looking in books and magazines for pictures of similarly sized and decorated rooms. Try loosening up in a small room or one that you don't spend much time in, like a guest bedroom or the powder room. If even that's too big a leap, paint the back wall of a bookcase or a porch floor in an unexpected color. It's satisfying and liberating.

4

COLOR ROOM BY ROOM

Every room in your house is an opportunity for color. Each space has particular conditions that will influence color choices: how it functions, its architecture, its furnishings, who uses it most and at what time of day. A bright sunny kitchen will handle color far differently from a cozy study. But don't just make assumptions—spend time really looking at and being in your rooms. Then experiment and don't be afraid to push the boundaries. A vibrant palette can not only flatter a room but also lift your spirits and sometimes even change your whole outlook. But it doesn't take a big color to make a big difference. Subtle color is still color, and quiet combinations can be transformative. Grab a handful of color chips and seize the day.

Entry Halls and Stair Halls

These pass-through spaces play a pivotal role in setting the tone for your home, whether they are saying "Welcome back" after a long day or "Come on in" to visitors. Entry halls are often visible from a house's major rooms, such as the living room, and can therefore provide an opportunity for some visual whimsy. I've worked on lots of houses where we mainly used a palette of neutrals but

took advantage of the entry hall to pop in engaging, memorable colors.

If you live in a home with more than one story, you'll need to decide on a color for the stair hall. It's easier said than done. The continuous walls of a stair hall provide no good place to stop one wall color and start another. This means that the color you choose for the first-floor hall needs to work all the way up. And since it is visible from almost every room in the house, the stair hall's color needs to unify all the other hues used for a home's multiplicity of spaces. This doesn't mean you can't paint a stair hall a distinctive color. It just means that you will have to consider the color

relationships formed by all the spaces that connect to the hall.

I usually handle stair halls in one of two ways. The first approach is to consider them last. I initially focus instead on all the colors of the connecting rooms. Then I walk through every space that connects to the staircase and hallways. I study all the colors being considered and select a range of compatible shades to test for the "spine" of the house. The second approach is the reverse. If the stair hall is already furnished with such semi-permanent materials as stair runners or wallpaper, the palette of those elements drives the color choice of the adjoining rooms.

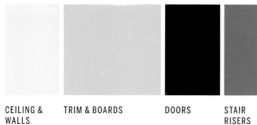

CEILING &
WALLS

TRIM & BOARDS

DOORS

STAIR
RISERS

The entryway in this mid-nineteenth-century Southern house was once dark and uninviting. To brighten the space while maintaining a sense of history, I used a pale sage green for the trim and the vertical beaded boards and painted the walls and the ceiling a creamy white. The stair risers are flat brown and the doors greenish-black, both colors typical of old houses in this region. Altogether, this palette creates a lighter space without making it look too "new."

Warm coffee-brown walls wrap black coat cubbies in this simple entryway. Easier to access than a traditional closet, as well as a clever use of small space, this mini-mudroom is a hardworking but attractive design solution. The black helps everything look tidy and doesn't show the "mud" part of the mudroom.

WALLS

CABINET

This photograph shows a small section of a very large staircase that travels up six stories in a town house. At first, my client wanted everything to be white. I suggested a slightly deeper limestone color for the insets of the dado panels as a way to make the space more interesting without veering too far away from the original all-white palette.

TRIM

INSET PANELS

The soft taupe walls in this entrance give way to a much brighter, creamy white living room. Beautiful custom mahogany doors and limestone floors are the real stars of this foyer. The paint color sits handsomely in the background, helping to showcase the materials. The envelope is simplified by painting the trim and the walls the same color.

FOYER WALLS   LIVING ROOM WALLS   ART

Several years ago I spent a long week in February painting and glazing green-on-green stripes up this staircase. The idea came from the homeowner, an amazing and precise architect. The process was arduous but the results beautiful. The vertical stripes echo the rhythm of the balusters and heighten the stair hall. The subtle contrast between the greens ensures that the pattern doesn't overpower the space.

STRIPE   STRIPE   CHAIR CUSHION

Living Rooms

Living rooms are typically the most formal space in the house, and usually the largest. As much as I love bold colors, it takes a good sense of proportion to make a big color statement in a large room. I often specify light, neutral colors for large rooms and make adjacent rooms more colorful. It's exciting for the eye to catch glimpses of color from the safety of a more temperate "home base."

Since the living room is where we tend to put our best face forward, many people get stymied when it comes to color because everything takes on more meaning. This is the room that is typically the showplace for our treasures, from furniture and art to rugs and antiques. While these design elements can drive the palette, a neutral hue that connects all your beautiful things is often the best way to go.

Occasionally I'll take a living room into bolder color territory. I was once called to look at the parlor in a town house in Brooklyn. The room was massive, with fourteen-foot ceilings and heavily contoured original moldings. The baseboards were fourteen inches tall. The proportions of the room were grand, but I was struck by the drabness of the space, which was painted a dull gray blue. The hue was tasteful but somehow killed the room's spirit.

Sure enough, when I asked the owners how much time they spent in their living room, they admitted that they rarely used it. Suddenly they realized that the sober wall color was largely to blame. I talked to them further about the way they lived, and I spent time looking at the architecture, furnishings, and lighting in the room. Finally it occurred to me that the big showy moldings needed something equally strong to hold on to—a real color, something distinct and confident. In the end we painted the walls a dark chocolate brown and the moldings a warm cream. The ceiling, a confection of plaster with a large central rosette, received a coat of sugary white. The room was transformed by a color scheme that mimicked an elegant European pastry—rich and delicious. Everybody loved it. Months later my clients called to tell me that the brown walls had changed the way they lived in their home and even compelled passersby to ring their bell to ask about the color. I really loved this experience because I felt that we had brought the room back to life by suiting it up in the right color.

It takes conviction to paint your living room walls orange! This pumpkin-colored room benefits greatly from its warm, inviting color. Offset by neutrals and browns, the walls are easy on the eyes and joyful all at once, making a bold but not overpowering statement.

WALLS   SOFA   OTTOMANS   RUG

A rich yellow creates a warm background for the dark woods and elegant textiles that furnish this comfortable, classic living room. The sisal rug and simple curtains are close in color to the walls. This lets the textures, colors, and patterns of the upholstery, pillows, art, and decorations create the room's character.

WALLS   TRIM   CEILING

The marine blue on the far wall of this living room, though muted, is a definite color statement. Together with the greener rug in a similar color weight, the blue creates an enveloping cocoon, absorbing the dark sofa and setting off a pair of prints. A chair in lemon yellow provides a lift, saving the space from succumbing to too somber a look.

WALLS   TRIM & CEILING   CHAIR FABRIC

A pale, soft wall color allows the warm tones of the wood sideboard and leather lounge chair to shine and serves as a neutral ground for a sophisticated composition of furnishings. An asymmetrical arrangement of photographs anchors one end of a narrow shelf reminiscent of the horizon line; the contours of the lounge chair layer graceful curves atop otherwise linear forms.

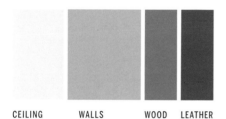

CEILING   WALLS   WOOD   LEATHER

You'd never know that this spacious bright room was once gloomy: boxed in by dark floors, old varnished trim, and faded wallpaper. By painting the trim and floors white and the walls a pale blue and then adding mid-century furnishings, the house's new owners completely transformed the look and feel of the room. Now it is tranquil and inviting. As they say, change is good. Sometimes a radical reimagining is the best way to bring new life to an old house.

WALLS   TRIM & CEILING   SOFA   CHAIR

Dining Rooms

Dining rooms lend themselves well to color. Used primarily in the evening, these rooms are often lit by the glow of sconces, chandeliers, and candles, which look wonderful within the context of richer hues. In fact, dining rooms benefit from a bit of drama. I was once in a remarkable dining room in Paris that had a white dado (the section of a wall between the baseboard and the chair rail) with

deep charcoal-gray walls above. It was amazing to see a table filled with candles against the dark backdrop. What's more, a wall color that recedes into the shadows at night places the guests at the table in the spotlight—which, as every good host knows, is how it should be.

Since a dining room is often visible from other rooms, consider how its color will look in that context. A deeply hued dining room contrasts nicely with a living room painted a quieter color.

A strong color draws the eye across space, especially when it's not competing with other bold hues. A subtler, more classic approach is to visually connect the dining and living rooms, particularly if they are adjacent, by using a similar color in each room (see "Sight Lines" on page 58). For instance, try painting a living room a warm yellow and an adjacent dining room a deeper gold.

WALLS **TRIM & CEILING** **ACCENT WALL**

In a large open space, a smart freestanding wall separates the dining room from the living area beyond. I intentionally kept the perimeter walls and ceiling quiet by painting them soft, light colors and chose a stronger neutral for the dividing wall. The camel color converses well with the multiple wood tones of the furniture and turns the wall into a pleasing focal point as well as an ideal place to feature art.

I love this bold orange wall. It creates drama as it separates the library from the rest of the loft. With bleached pine floors creating a continuous spacious feeling, the orange gives our eye a place to land in this big, open space. The distinct modern color holds its own against mid-century chairs upholstered in black and brings an old portrait to life.

WALL   FLOOR

The cheerful yellow that covers the old plaster walls of this small dining room serves as a visual bridge between old wood beams and crisp white trim. The color makes the space warm and inviting day and night. Vibrant blue objects atop a graphic fireplace complement the yellow in this playful room.

WALLS   ACCENT

One Palette, Two Rooms

These dining rooms have much in common despite the differences in their architectural styles. In the traditional room on the right, painting everything (walls, trim, ceiling) white modernizes the space by enhancing its volume rather than the surface details. The room feels as open and bright as the contemporary room on the left. Both rooms get lots of natural light, have minimal window treatments, and are anchored by dark satin-finished floors. You can see what a big difference a light-colored rug makes in contrast to the sleek, uncovered floor in the modern loft. In the traditional room, white appears warmer, more "aged," if you will, than it does in the cooler, more "modern" loft.

WALLS   WOOD

Kitchens

When I look at colors for kitchens, I start by looking at the materials. Kitchens are rooms with a lot of different surfaces and textures bumping into one another. Beautiful stone slabs or handmade tiles can be quite bossy, almost deciding the wall color for you. And they should; they cost a lot more than paint. So look to them for color ideas. Pull a hue from a marble counter—not just from the

overall color but from its veining—or from wood grain. Consider grout a color opportunity. Beyond white, there are dozens of ready-mixed colors available. A darker grout like pale gray not only looks good but also doesn't show the dirt.

Kitchens are such hives of activity that you don't want to overload the senses with too much color, but a little bit is always fun. Many cooks have colorful collections—of copper pots, dishware, and cookbooks—and like to have their cookware exposed for easy accessibility. In such cases, I often use the wall color as a backdrop. Blocks of color can turn normal kitchen clutter like pots and pans into interesting displays. In a kitchen with glass-fronted cabinets, for instance, try painting the interior a cheerful hue.

Not surprisingly, many kitchens are predominantly white. White helps reflect light sources and enhances our ability to see, which is a matter of safety as well as convenience. In general, white is tidy and lends a feeling of spaciousness. But for an all-white kitchen to really dazzle, nearly every component has to be pristine and of the same white. A mix of whites close in value but not in hue (that is, some warm, some cool) makes for a haphazard look. This doesn't mean you can't combine white with other light neutral colors; just remember to keep them in the same family—warm white with tan, cool white with gray.

WALLS

WOOD

For this new country kitchen, I chose an apple green for the walls. To give the appearance of old farmhouse walls, I first had the contractor hand-trowel plaster onto them. The painters then applied paint with wide brushes, replicating old methods. The sense of age and weight provides a contrast to the sleek stainless-steel kitchen components, while the cheerful green walls set off the warm woods that make up the floors, cabinets, windows, trim, and furniture.

Friends of mine have one of those center-of-the-universe kitchens— always filled with activity. Kids, dogs, visitors, *and* clients (the room is used in photo shoots) all figure into the daily picture. To manage this cacophony, the front of the refrigerator has a panel coated with chalkboard paint to create a large message board. Black cabinets frame the fridge and rim the large room in a counter-height band. The walls and lofty ceiling are a pale beach-glass green, enhancing the spaciousness.

WALLS   CHALKBOARD

A classic country kitchen sits calmly next to a tangerine-walled dining room, looking quiet by comparison. That's often the trick when it comes to employing a bold, bossy color like bright orange. If you want a room to be a central focal point, paint it an eye-catching color and the surrounding rooms in more subtle shades. Don't forget that the neutral rooms may pick up, via reflection, some of the stronger color.

DINING ROOM   KITCHEN   CABINETS
WALLS   WALLS

In this predominantly white loft space I selected two medium grays to define the open-plan kitchen. Two columns of gray cabinets echo the vertical vent shaft of the stove hood, helping to keep the hood from seeming adrift. The same gray lends the island weight. Adding a subtle color to a space like this gives it a little distinction without fighting the cohesive spirit of the loft.

CABINETS   FLOWERS

This modest kitchen makes great use of white to create a spacious, unified feeling. Beneath the white countertop, the dishwasher and the half-height refrigerator and freezer fit right into the band of white lower cabinets. If you want to blend simple white appliances into your cabinets, get several white paint chips and see which is the closest match. Use this white for the cabinet doors to unify all the surfaces. A reduced palette allows the eye to scan the bright room with ease, giving us a sense of openness and simplicity.

CABINETS   WALLS

Utility Spaces

Garages, basements, storage areas, and closets don't have to be color afterthoughts. Instead of giving them the usual coat of serviceable white or gray, do something inspired. I had a friend who painted the inside of his garage like an Hermès box—orange walls, chocolate-brown window and door frames, brown banding in the "seams" of the room, and a big, brown *H* on the back wall. It looked

sensational and was a crazy surprise behind the garage door.

Color can really lift spirits in a less-than-beautiful utilitarian space. The basement of my prewar apartment building used to be typical of its era: lots of old pipes and wires, cement floors painted battleship gray, flat white walls with fluorescent tubes casting dull light. Beyond uninviting, it was depressing. When the basement was renovated, I was surprised to find all of the trim and doors painted Creamsicle orange. It was thrilling that someone else in my building recognized color's capacity to cheer.

I've lost track of how many times I've specified color for the interiors of closets. It's a color addition that's so satisfying because it's relatively simple and utterly transforming. I once worked on a pristine white town house owned by a fashion stylist who asked me to help him find a meaningful way to introduce color. He showed me his closets (something my clients rarely do), which were curated like displays in a beautiful shop. They seemed like the perfect place for a color, so we chose one of his favorites—Wedgwood blue—as the backdrop to his magnificent collection of suits, ties, shoes, and hats.

Painting a nice color inside a closet seems to help us keep it organized. Maybe figuring out the color also helps us to figure out how to use the space. Just be sure your closet is well lit before opting to paint it a dark color.

I am a big fan of putting uplifting colors in utilitarian spaces. A lemony yellow takes this laundry room to a new level. *Cheerful, vibrant,* and *inviting* are not words many of us can use to describe the area that contains our washer and dryer! Even if you don't have a laundry room per se, try painting the wall behind the machines an unexpected color.

WALLS   CABINETS   CURTAIN

This series of distinct colors moves from a persimmon open pantry to a sliver of apple-green kitchen wall and into a golden-yellow foyer, all framed by natural fir. Since the pantry is small and mostly lined with shelving, it can hold on to a big, lively color without the color being overpowering. Indeed, a room glimpsed only in passing is an opportunity to use color to intrigue and please, since it is seen fleetingly and from an angle. And strong color makes a nice backdrop for attractive product packaging.

WALL   WALL   WALL

Home Offices

People have different ideas about the kind of environment they need in order to be productive and creative. Some like bright rooms; others prefer to hole up in a dark space. For some the kitchen table will do, but most people who work from home benefit from a dedicated office space where color can play an important part in supporting their work efforts.

I've found that people have very specific requirements for their work areas. An artist friend says he's most productive at a white table with a laminate top—he likes the way the pen "bounces" on that particular surface. His studio ended up an ethereal gray. A writer friend needed the brightest room possible—painted Super White—in order to get anything done. One client appreciates his walnut-paneled study for its cavelike quality, saying he feels sealed in and focused; I selected a pale pumpkin color for his ceiling to harmonize with the wood walls and tartan wool upholstery. In one family's beach house, we nicknamed the husband's den Man World (even the contractors called it that), as if it were a serious architectural term. The handsome taupe walls were a complete departure from the otherwise light palette of the house, as were the bays of the bookcases, for which I chose random colors from nautical flags.

A longtime client and friend has her home office tucked into a closet. Once you open the door, an opulent, personal world appears. Everything is coral colored—the walls, the desktop, and the shelves. On the inside of the door is a bulletin board jammed with memorabilia, photos, and notes. The shelves are filled with even more color—magazines, books, and robin's-egg-blue boxes. This kind of visual stimulation would drive some people right over the edge, but she couldn't be happier. Being surrounded by her favorite things inspires her.

Many of us have an ongoing love affair with the color of natural Belgian linen. The taupey greige tone seems to always look right as the background for collections. It gives walls more gravity than white but remains neutral enough to stand behind just about anything. I particularly love dark woods, creams, and whites with it. In this home office, it's a calm backdrop to a lot of visual activity. Bright yellow flowers provide a welcome shot of color.

WALLS

FRAMES

FLOWERS

This architect's home office is a tranquil respite from his fever-pitched daily workplace. We chose a warm caramel beige for the walls and black office furniture to anchor the room. His watercolors look serene hanging above the long desk. I love how the light from the window travels across the wall, illuminating them.

WALLS   DESK & CHAIR

This home office is a great example of how to use a bold color like bright turquoise in palatable doses. I love how the color is a little bit different from piece to piece and how the pale green walls pull it all together. This is the kind of color combination that begs for even more color. It's easy to imagine other blues, greens, pinks, and reds piling on.

WALLS   FABRIC   FURNITURE

A large landscape painting in lush blues and greens acts like a dramatic window behind my client's desk. Pale buttery-white walls wrap around the corner, making the office area bright and allowing the painting to be the focal point. A big bunch of flowers always sits on the desktop, bringing a burst of bold color into the mix.

WALLS   PAINTING   FLOWERS

A good friend of mine sits at her Shaker desk reading and writing e-mails and taking breaks to gaze out the window at her llamas, which gather at the gate and look back to see what she's doing. Tucked in the corner of a large country kitchen, this cozy office area is perfectly located in the hub of the house. The butter-yellow leather chair was chosen for comfort and for color—she loves how the walls, woods, and chair work together to create her niche.

WALLS   WOOD   CHAIR

Master Bedrooms

In addition to providing a place to sleep, the bedroom is a private space where we retreat to think, read, relax, dream, and get away from the bustle of family life. Since the master bedroom or suite is self-contained, color choices don't necessarily have to work directly with other areas of the living space. We are free to make our bedroom colors romantic, soothing, or dramatic.

I've been surprised by several of my clients' ideas for their bedrooms. Bright red walls are more popular than I would have imagined. My tendency is to go for relaxing colors that aren't going to keep people up at night or challenge the eye first thing in the morning. But my idea of relaxing might be someone else's double Valium of boredom. I like talking with my clients about how they want to feel when they are in their room. Some people use their bedrooms only for sleeping, while others furnish theirs with desks, televisions (and TV trays for snacking), laptops, and books. The way you use this room will help you choose colors for it.

Darkly colored bedrooms can be sexy and beautiful at night. But it's worth considering the potentially jarring effect of bright morning light; the high contrast can be very uncomfortable for the eyes. If you do decide to go for a deep color, invest in blackout shades and good window treatments so you can wake up peacefully. Keep in mind too that just because you've opted for a deep wall color, it doesn't mean everything else has to fall into darkness. To me, white sheets are a lot more appealing than brown ones. And light-colored bed linens, as well as other furnishings like curtains and carpeting, are an easy way to strike a happy balance between dark and light.

| WALLS | FLOOR | PLANTS |

This master bedroom is about three colors—white, amber yellow, and green. The walls, ceiling, and trim are all painted the same white to form a simple envelope. The warm amber hue of reclaimed wide-plank pine floors is only occasionally interrupted by small flat-weave rugs. Green foliage is always present but ever changing in this landscape architect's bedroom. At times the plants are so alive that they seem to infuse the air with color. The white walls act as a blank canvas for the verdant greens.

Color transforms this small room by giving it a distinct and memorable personality. With barely enough space for a bed, a small desk, and a side chair, this little room could be less than inviting. But the rich robin's-egg-blue wall color creates such a pleasant atmosphere that it compels a visit. Plus it's a nice sight-line color from the hallway. The mirror and the white-painted beamed ceiling help brighten and open the room to create a more spacious feeling.

WALLS   CEILING

The wall color in this classic room is what many of my clients refer to as "paper bag." Right up there with Belgian linen, paper bag is one of those attractive, all-purpose colors that has a fan club. Also touted as "camel" and "caramel," the warm shade works beautifully in this kind of traditional decor, bringing natural woods and neutral fabrics together in a tone-on-tone family.

WALLS   FABRIC

Dark window frames and shades form vertical columns that help lift the height of this top-floor bedroom. Painting the low ceiling white both brightens the space and reinforces the band effect of the wall color, a pleasing French blue that gives the room a sense of place and distinction.

WALLS   TRIM

Soft yellow walls set a tranquil tone for this master bedroom. The pale wall-to-wall carpet contributes to a sense of spaciousness, as do the sheer linen Roman blinds. The light gray of the club chair and ottoman complements the yellow and echoes the hue of the closet doors. Even the deep eggplant of the bedcover is somehow soft. As a whole, the room's color palette works to soothe all who enter.

WALLS   BED   CHAIR

Children's Rooms

My attitude toward kids' rooms is: if you can't beat 'em, join 'em. I enjoy asking children about their favorite colors because they are usually fearless and instinctual. My goal is to find cool, fun colors that the kids like and the parents can tolerate. The thirteen-year-old son of one of my clients reported that his favorite color was Citibank blue, as in the bright corporate logo. Within the context of a

lovely old farmhouse his mother was updating, I set out to make the loud blue a palatable reality. It became the trim in his room, nicely framing periwinkle walls and a pale blue ceiling.

One of my favorite small clients, Juliet, is the only second grader I know with more than two hundred books (her mom is an author). Juliet has a rabid love of every hue, especially pink. For her small Manhattan bedroom, I started with bright white walls to make the most of limited natural light. Then came color—pink, green, and sky blue—in the form of big vinyl polka dots affixed to the walls. To add some fun to the bookshelves, we mixed in stuffed animals, toy figures and cars, family photos, and bins holding art supplies.

A happy medium is to put colors inside closets and on the ceiling. I had a client who was opposed to having color on the walls in his impeccably white house. So I painted the son's room white—but gave it a lime-green ceiling and a grass-green closet interior. His sister got a pale pink ceiling and a closet lined in fuchsia and red. That closet was so bright and brimming with toys that it was as if bells and horns sounded whenever the closet doors were opened.

It can be a lot of fun to focus on what interests my junior clients. For budding artists I'll suggest chalkboard paint for a wall or a door. In a basement playroom I used a vibrant color wheel palette, making each of the walls a different bright color. A basketball fan has a miniature court painted on his floor. There are endless and entertaining options for enlivening children's bedrooms or play spaces, many of them easy and affordable.

STRIPED WALLS

ACCENT

Wide stripes of pale yellow and warm white make this young girl's room playful with a hint of sophistication. The striped carpet paired with floral fabrics creates a come-one-come-all invitation to more pattern and color, as does a mix of landscape and still-life paintings. Children's rooms are a great place for a variety of colors and textures.

I've never met a kid who didn't like a secret hideaway or a cozy corner for drifting off into make-believe. This little niche is kitted out with pink and blue floral prints and a small tucked-away wall of snapshots. The rest of the room is soft white and pale pink, letting the bolder colors inhabit the bed alcove.

WALLS   WALL FABRIC

This girl's room employs a fail-safe technique for dealing with the ever-changing tastes of a child. When virtually everything is painted white, the room becomes a blank slate for whimsy and short-term color statements. An orangey pink inside the bookcases does the heavy lifting for color in the room. The bedding, posters, and other bits and pieces can freely change, altering the look of the room easily and dramatically.

INSIDE   WALLS   FABRIC
BOOKCASE

Who says a baby's room has to be pastel? Not only is a strong color, like this tomato red, stimulating to young eyes, it's a good foil for baby furnishings, which tend to be light in tone. Here, large paintings temper the wall color and contribute far-from-infantile yet playful pattern, as do a hooked rug and a life-size zebra.

ACCENT WALL   OTHER WALLS   BLANKET ART

Twin boys get a set of fire-engine-red steel lockers, sturdy bunk beds, a floor painted a deeper red, and chalkboard-painted walls. It's a bombproof room for boy action. Since the classic blackboard color is so deep, it's perfect to pair with bold, bright colors like the red lockers. Pile in the multicolored fabrics and toys; this room can handle it.

CHALKBOARD WALLS   FLOOR   LOCKERS

Guest Rooms

A guest room is the perfect place to employ a design scheme that you love but don't want to live with 24/7. I like to think of my guest room as a gift to my visitors, and I try to create a comfortable, relaxing, and memorable environment for them. It's also a laboratory for my ideas. I might paint a landscape mural on one wall just for the fun of it, or use the walls to test colors that intrigue me.

I feel like I can change the room whenever I want to because its whole function is about transience. One of my favorite memories is of a very small hotel room in Paris. The ceiling was white, but every other surface was painted in a rich cream high-sheen lacquer. The glossy paint made the light glint and dance around the tiny room. While small in scale, the room felt luminous and special.

Many of us have space restrictions that make maintaining a room solely for guests difficult, if not impossible. And too often the guest bedroom becomes a repository for hand-me-down furnishings, as well as the storage area for bulky items like suitcases and sports equipment. I often advise my clients to make the guest bedroom a multipurpose room from the start so that it functions well and looks good all the time. Disparate furnishings can be transformed into a cohesive suite of furniture with a coat of paint and some new upholstery or slipcovers. For my guest bedroom in the country I have dedicated one of the closets to general household items and left a smaller closet for guests. I also keep a lot of art supplies there so guests feel encouraged to dabble along with me—country air can make a person feel creative!

This guest nook, graced with a few carefully selected details, is quiet and dramatic all at once. Located in the hallway in a loftlike house, the niche accommodates an occasional guest on a homespun-draped bed, tucked behind a linen folding screen when the lights go out. The soft white walls keep the small alcove bright and open and showcase the linear forms of natural branches, wall lights (sconce and sconce jr.), and a tattersall pillow cover.

WALLS

PILLOW
FABRIC

Pale gray and natural whites in shades of linen and ivory lend this urban bedroom an atmosphere of total serenity. Though sharper in tone, the pure white bed linens project comfort that's clean and fresh.

WALLS

CURTAINS

TRIM

Bathrooms

Many people use their master bathroom as a sanctuary from the pressures that lurk beyond the door. For this reason, a light palette—which helps with visibility and looks clean—is usually the best choice. That being said, in certain situations a homeowner wants a more colorful master bathroom. Color can help set a mood and make the room a distinctly private and personal space.

If you are renovating or building a bathroom from scratch, try this approach: Gather small samples of all of the materials used in the bathroom, from tile to marble to hardware. Assemble them together on a board or tray that you can move around and look at under different lighting conditions. This is very helpful for choosing paint colors. Add paint sample cards to your materials palette and spend time looking at how all of the elements work together. You are searching for a subtle color that works in concert with your space, whether it is filled with stone, tile, mirror, glass, metal, or wood. If you're working with existing surfaces and fixtures, you'll need to take your color chips and tests into the bathroom and look at them along with the rest of the materials.

Many of my clients are concerned about moisture in bathrooms and worry that it will damage a paint job. This is no longer a major concern. While ventilation in a bathroom is always important, today's paint will hold up just fine in almost any finish. It's no longer necessary to paint the bathroom in semi- or high-gloss oil paint or to avoid outfitting your bathroom with softer, natural materials. In fact, treating the bathroom as "furnishable" can be a great design approach. Adding elements like a mirror framed in wood, an interesting side chair, a real rug (not just a bath mat), and prints on the wall warms up a space that can sometimes feel cold. And if these elements are in darker tones, they ground a room that may be, due to its light palette, at risk of seeming adrift.

For a new but remarkably built Georgian house, I worked hard to bring a lot of strong color into the overall palette without pushing the elegant home past its comfort zone. These bathroom walls are a saturated ochre yellow that looks beautiful behind the gilt-edged mahogany mirror. The bold color is balanced by the satin-white wainscoting that bands the lower half of the room.

WALLS

SINK

ACCENT

Artwork of similar size, all in dark frames with wide mattes, creates a graphic "wallpaper" for a high-ceilinged bathroom. The pale dove-gray wall color picks up on the marble counter and trim while the pool-blue tile provides the leading color and a textural balance to the artwork.

TILE WALLS FRAMES

This is a classic combination: pale pink walls with clean white trim. I love how the large fans of coral punch past the pink into a distinct color of their own. This soft palette is easy on the eyes and flattering to everyone. And it allows for just about any accent color for towels and art.

TOWELS WAINSCOTING UPPER WALL

Many bathrooms are almost completely covered with tile or stone. In this case, dark slate tiles line the floors and three quarters of the walls, creating a moody but tranquil environment. A pale limestone color is painted above to add light while still being compatible with the stone below. The large mirror becomes a focal point and a source of illumination for the space.

WALLS &   TILE   FRAME
CEILING

Ample daylight from this bathroom's large window, extended by mirrors, balances the dark chocolate brown of its walls, an extension of the bedroom color beyond. Ivory trim and continuous sisal carpeting further unite the two rooms as a suite.

WALLS   TRIM   SISAL FLOOR

Powder Rooms

If you are fortunate enough to have a powder room or a small guest bath, then you have a great opportunity to do something daring with color. These tiny spaces can be treated like jewel boxes to be filled with treasure—beautiful fixtures, antique wallpaper, gilded ceilings, fanciful mirrors, eclectic or unusual objects, and unexpected color. I have worked on several projects where we chose

patterned wallpaper for the powder room because it could add more vibrancy than a single paint color (and in a small space, you don't need a lot of wallpaper rolls to cover the walls).

I've worked on some very colorful powder rooms in homes with otherwise neutral or limited palettes. For a client in New York, I concocted a secret red room, as she called it, for her powder room. Having worked on her house in East Hampton the previous summer, I knew that she had a penchant for rich, earthy colors. When I arrived at her new city place, the austerity of the color scheme surprised me. "I'm being ruled by

architects," she whispered to me at our first site meeting, in the midst of what was still a messy renovation. "Help me get a color into this apartment—please!" From that point on we two coconspirators snuck around with color chips while the architects talked shop with the contractors. Once the dust finally settled and the acres of "architect white" had dried, my client had her favorite red lacquered onto the walls of the powder room, a place so well hidden that it was located behind a false wall—no guest could find it without directions. It was a tremendous and memorable surprise.

I tested my own color Field in my powder room in the country. The view from the window is a swirl of green, and I wanted to see what it would be like to bring some of that color indoors. And it works—the walls of mirror and green actually feel like an extension of the fields outside. Of course it helps that, given the house's isolation, window coverings are not a priority.

WALLS   STEEL SHELF

Behind the door to this powder room lies a big surprise. The rest of the house is fairly quiet—sedate, even—making the visual activity of this room all the more unexpected. Not only is the daring wallpaper colorful, it's boldly scaled, especially for a small room. And why stop at wallpaper? Hang art on top of it! These little rooms are perfect for an outburst of design fun.

WALLPAPER

5

CASE STUDIES: EVE ON SITE

I've had the great fortune to work with some remarkably talented architects and designers. I've also been blessed with a roster of clients who have included me in exciting and challenging projects. And although I'm not a client, I'm constantly experimenting with color, using my own spaces as testing labs. What follows is a broad sampling of projects that I've been involved with, from grand to humble, historic to modern, in the city and in the countryside. If there is one thing that unites them all, it's taking the time to become familiar with a place and its conditions and then testing, testing, testing.

Urban Loft 1

I have worked with my good friend and colleague interior designer Martin Raffone on several challenging projects over the years. Martin is a visionary when it comes to organizing space and creating atmosphere, particularly in open-plan spaces such as lofts, in which a subtle palette can be used to unify and define varying zones.

For most people, this loft—a former industrial space on Mercer Street in Manhattan—would have been a nonstarter. It was long and narrow with three windows at the front end and one at the rear. The layout was awkward, and the lighting was gloomy on the sunniest day. The homeowner, a young guy from California in the music business, was used to the beach, sun, and nature. This was to be his New York outpost, a space where he could work and host parties for his East Coast friends and industry colleagues.

Drawing on the idea of the shore and the outdoors, Martin had the idea of creating a kind of "urban beach" scheme. He designed a system of horizontal wood-plank paneling that ringed the periphery of the loft, defining seating areas and passageways. We worked together to come up with a driftwood-like stain for all of the wood. The gray stain unified the distinct areas that Martin had crafted with the planking and made the loft's boxcar layout into a series of well-considered, usable spaces for sitting, dining, sleeping, working, and cooking. Moreover, the weathered palette really softened the big space. I mixed the water-based stain in my studio in a five-gallon container, which became known simply as the Big Bucket and was carted from spot to spot in the loft for staining not only all of the wood but also a big patch of plaster wall.

One afternoon early on in the project, the client arrived at the loft with a beautiful photograph by the artist Clay Ketter. The photo depicted an old brick building whose exterior carried the

Left: A view looking toward the front of the loft space. The sheer shades on the three windows facing onto the narrow streets of SoHo let in as much light as possible. The satin-finish black floors reflect light into the room, and artificial light is used to enhance the effect.

Opposite: A Zen-like view of a simple wooden stool perched in front of a painted brick wall. The overhead lights enhance the texture of the white bricks by creating deeper shadows.

ghostly outline of its since-demolished neighbor, a powerful image that alluded to history and the passage of time. The photograph inspired us to leave a big expanse of old plaster and brick intact and openly visible in the renovated loft. Martin had the contractors carefully sand parts of the plaster to make the old wall look more artful. Then we used the Big Bucket to stain it, pulling old and new together so the photograph and the loft space told the same story of life and change in urban places.

For the floor, we developed a dark stain that helped both ground the expansive space and disguise a century of industrial wear and tear. It preserved the history of the loft while elevating it to a refined residence. For the ceiling and many of the walls we used basic white. It was the perfect, simple contrast to the textures and materials—clean, modern, and uneventful, which allowed the handsome paneling and furnishings to take center stage.

Soon after the loft was completed, the owner hosted a big party to introduce his friends to his new digs and to celebrate its successful completion. We watched as people filtered in, oohing and aahing in the soft, beautifully lit space. I loved seeing the guests mill around, their eyes slowly moving over all of the subtle textures and colors while their hands casually ran over the old brick, plaster, and wood surfaces. The real lesson from this project for me was that any space, even one with a gritty past, can be radically transformed and made not only livable but also urbane and sophisticated.

Above: This view looks back through the loft to the kitchen. An old plaster wall sits in the middle of the space on the left, while driftwood-colored paneling and shelving span the right. Neutral tones let the eye wander slowly down the long, open room.

Right: The original plaster wall looks like a grand abstract canvas behind this sculptural chair. By carefully preserving a section of the old wall, we brought random textural gestures to an otherwise orderly series of surfaces. The effect was painterly and compelling.

Above: Mark Huddleston's wonderful photograph of the seating area captures the quality of light and color in the loft post-renovation. The angle and the light remind me of Renaissance paintings. Martin's keen sense of composition with the furnishings adds to the timeless beauty.

Urban Loft 2

My second project with Martin Raffone was a newly renovated space in a former chain factory. Unlike the Mercer Street loft, which was raw and unfurnished, this space had pristine surfaces, and the owners, who were collectors of mid-century modern furniture and objects, already had plenty of furnishings. A previous decorator had installed sheer curtains, carpets, and a few other elements

before Martin and I arrived on the scene. Martin considered this job a "decorating fix," one where we would swoop in and rescue, remove, re-arrange, and make sense of what was already there and needed to stay.

One of the first things we discussed was how the architecture, in spite of a few bold gestures like different ceiling levels and some large columns, lacked distinction, especially in the entry-way and adjacent hall gallery. Determined to maintain a subtle palette and work quietly with

the architecture, I chose a deep gray that coordi-nated with the metallic gray tiles in the kitchen's prominent backsplash. I applied the color selec-tively, using it on several columns to give them definition and separate them from the white walls.In the corner of the kitchen, I painted a column and the adjoining ceiling with the gray, along with the ceiling in the hall. A nice cocoa brown on the hall's end wall created a discreet focal point. The remainder of the loft stayed white. Martin calls this approach "using color selectively to clarify the architecture." That is exactly what it did, subtly but very effectively. The message here is that small moves, colorwise, can create big changes in your home. You don't always have to redecorate everything to alter the look of your space.

Left: I chose a medium stone-gray color in the hallway to diminish the scale of nonremovable columns and make the ceiling recede. Since the architecture is planar and without much detail, Martin decided to use art, materials, and fabrics to bring small doses of color and texture into the loft.

Opposite, below: Most of the loft is white, but I used gray judiciously to define and enhance the architecture. The kitchen is anchored by a wide rectangular column of gray in the corner. The gray also travels between the ceiling and the cabinets and across the face of the return where the ceiling drops over the kitchen. These subtle shifts help to make areas of the large open plan feel considered and purposeful.

Left: The color shifts are very subtle in this loft, almost more felt than seen. I painted the entrance dark gray to push the space back, help define it, and create a different feeling from the brighter hallway.

A Historic House in Charleston

When architect Gil Schafer first contacted me about a project in Charleston, South Carolina, it was already under way. Built in 1840, the grand brick house had survived the Civil War, an earthquake, several hurricanes, and tenants known for their wild parties. Now the house was being transformed through a distinguished renovation. I've worked with Gil on many projects and appreciate

his tireless energy and elegant perfectionism. This project would also introduce me to Charleston-based contractor-restorer extraordinaire Richard Marks.

When I first arrived at the house in the heart of the city's historic district, I was greeted by a swarm of skilled workmen—plasterers, wood carvers, stonemasons, electricians, plumbers, painters, and landscapers—all crisscrossing from room to room and passing one another on the many flights of stairs, carrying buckets, pipes, lumber, stone, tile, tools, panes of glass, ladders, and lunch. My first meeting with Richard was at a dusty Formica-topped caterer's table that had been set up in the middle of the grand dining room. Beige folding chairs were scattered around, and boxed lunches

sat in stacks next to floor plans and paint decks. Richard introduced himself as "Moby" and began outlining the project's scope in his congenial Southern manner. In addition to being a repository of local lore, Moby possessed a mind-boggling amount of information about history, materials, and methods. We discussed how homes age, the "expiration dates" of the parts and pieces, and how to go about the task of bringing new life to an old house.

In addition to specifying color, my role was to advise on the methods used to restore the walls and wood surfaces, making them ready for paint. I took the time to learn the house, floor by floor, room by room, to think about how the spaces would be used, which parts of the house would be

Left: While the exterior of this historic brick house doesn't seem too driven by color, there were numerous color considerations involved in the restoration. We discussed and selected colors for mortar, flashing, shutters (Charleston Green), porch floors and ceilings, hinges and downspouts.

Opposite: It's hard to beat Charleston for grand old houses that sit cheek by jowl in the historic part of town. This house emanates history as you walk its gracious rooms. I chose a color called Rhett Pumpkin for the generous stair hall. It's the first thing you see when you open the front door, and it winds its way up to the top, setting the tone for the whole house.

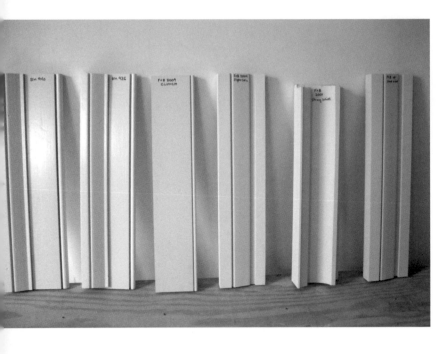

Above left: I asked the painters to make samples of trim in our test colors, which I then clearly labeled with a marker.

Left: The trim samples allowed us to freely move through the house, examining test colors in concert with wall colors and wallpapers. Here, I am trying out a trim color in the dining room.

Above: Knowing that the dining room would be lined in a wallpaper mural guided our color choices for the adjacent rooms. Three large blocks of color painted on a wall of the middle parlor helped us determine which was the best complement to the wallpaper sample tacked up in the distance.

Opposite: The freshly painted parlor rooms look elegant despite the minimal furnishings. The slight shift in color, with the lighter room in the distance, helps create a greater sense of space.

public and which private, and most important, how color could be used to support the history, architecture, and attitude of the house. Working closely with Gil, I started to develop a concept for the main parlor floor. Gil presented three versions of a pattern of hand-blocked scenic wallpaper under consideration for the dining room. We chose one variation, which made selecting colors for the adjacent rooms much easier. We tested several versions of a rich, golden yellow, a color that related to the warm tones in the wallpaper, before we settled on the right hue.

As the color plan unfolded for the interior spaces, it became clear that the house held color well. Bold colors felt appropriate and provided striking backgrounds for the owner's impressive collection of antique American furniture. Even though serious research had been done about the materials used to build the house and careful attention was being paid to the methods of restoration, we did not feel hemmed in by the real or imagined constraints of historical precedent with regard to color. After all, this project was a private residence, not a collection of period rooms.

Yet sometimes historical colors can be striking. One of the biggest decisions was what color to paint the entry and stair hall, which was four stories tall. I could just hear the noble house begging for something distinctive, and it must have been speaking loudly because Gil tossed out the idea of orange. Moby gave us a copy of the Historic Colors of Charleston paint chart, and there was the perfect hue: Rhett Pumpkin. Not a color for the timid, this deep grayed orange gave the house a distinct character—bold, warm, and inviting—as it wound its way up the stair hall.

My role as color consultant extended well beyond the walls, as it often does on a project of this complexity. On the exterior, I weighed in on the colors for gutters, chimney flashing, shutters, porch floors, the loggia ceiling, and the mortar for repointing; inside, I worked out a palette that took in the stairs risers, pieces of handrails, cabinets, even the grout between tiles. Slowly, with skill and thoughtfulness, the Charleston house came together, reborn as a twenty-first-century beauty with great respect for the past.

The Relevance of Historic Colors

Historically significant, antique, or vintage houses pose an interesting issue with respect to color selection, both inside and out. How important is it that we adhere to a historically accurate color palette? Should we approach our homes as if they were sacred archaeological sites, carefully chipping through the layers to determine whether the hallway was originally green or brown? Despite all our technical advances, we still can't always determine what historical colors actually looked like. Many paint companies' lines of "historic" paints are only interpretations of true period colors.

Just as we don't wear eighteenth-century frocks in our Colonial house or prepare kettles of stew from historically accurate recipes, we shouldn't feel pressured to re-create the past when it comes to color. The modern world has brought us brighter lighting, endless color options in paint and materials, larger windows, and better insulation. All of these factors influence how we use and decorate our homes. My process when choosing colors for an old house is the same one I use for a new house—listen to the environment, look at the architecture, study how the light affects the spaces, and consider how the occupants use the rooms. Though my choices for a historical house respect the past, they are always firmly rooted in the here and now.

Opposite: The finished house has open, spacious rooms on the parlor floor. I wanted to support the wonderful mural and let it steal the show in the main part of the house, so I chose warm, subordinate colors for all the adjacent rooms.

Left: All of the trim in the main part of the house is the same color—a soft white that's neither too bright and new-looking nor too creamy—because I wanted a degree of contrast with the warmer wall colors.

Below: The large kitchen sits in the original service wing of the house, at the back of the property. Here, I changed direction with the color palette, shifting from warmer colors in the main rooms of the house to cooler ones that seemed appropriate for a kitchen in a southern climate. The cabinetry and paneling are all satin-finish sage green, while the walls are a soft white with sage and cream undertones.

My City Home

I've been getting to know my New York City living room for almost twenty years, and we still argue. Don't get me wrong—I love my apartment, in a classic Manhattan prewar building, for its substantial walls, handsome moldings, and high ceilings. But the space also has several issues that I am constantly contending with, including an odd arrangement of doors and a northern exposure, which

can feel a bit shadowy and lacking in warmth. For the longest time I went with a pale, warm gray for the walls, figuring since I couldn't overrule the cool, low natural light, I might as well go along for the dull ride. But boredom eventually won out and I painted a moss-green rectangle on the largest wall and used it as a backdrop for a large mirror and several of my own paintings. That worked for a while—until I decided to get rid of a

bunch of furniture. Then it was back to the drawing board. Next I went for a brighter white for everything—trim, walls, and ceiling. The room looked more modern and seamless. But, being me, I had to try something else. I brushed out a small wall in dark gray chalkboard paint and then put a silver mica drip finish over it, which was subtle but added a little glimmer. But I couldn't stop there, so I painted a three-foot-high band of violet along a wall where I park bicycles, because I liked how the bikes looked in front of it. I have no doubt that as time passes and my life and ideas change, my apartment will change too.

I've lost count of the various incarnations of color and decoration that have blown through. I'm still fighting with the northern exposure, flip-flopping between light and dark colors to buck or enhance the dull indirect light. Currently the bedroom is white, the small connecting hall is red, and the kitchen is cream and gray.

I've always loved the artist Paul Klee's description of a drawing as "simply a line going for a walk." Late one night that idea inspired me to take a line for a really long stroll. I took a round quarter-inch paintbrush and some cream paint and painted a linear pattern on the chartreuse walls and ceiling in my foyer. My guess is that by the time this book hits the shelves, many of these walls will be sporting new colors and finishes. Bottom line: there is no reason that a color scheme has to be static.

Opposite: A view into my kitchen with its lower band of chalkboard paint. To the right of the door frame, notice the band of purple that runs along one wall of the living room.

Below: In my entry hall I used a creamy white paint thinned with water so that it flowed easily from my watercolor brush. I painted an endless freehand line over the entire surface. Everyone thinks it's wallpaper until I tell them the truth!

Above: Sometimes a wall just needs a bit more life, especially if it lives in a shadowy part of the house. Adding sparkle is easy. My silver mica drip finish is a mixture of Golden brand interference paints (translucent acrylics that contain flecks of colored mica—think eye shadow), available at art supply stores, mixed with water to create a "drippable" consistency. I use an inch-wide brush to layer my mixture in a band across the top of a wall and let drips run down the surface to the floor. The intensity of the finish depends on how many layers I apply.

My Country Home

I think my city apartment was probably relieved when I built a house in the country and it started getting all my attention. I had somewhere else to paint and so many new things to apply it to. Shifting from a Manhattan apartment to a small, modern house situated in the middle of a large meadow also presented me with a new set of conditions. At last I had light-filled rooms to work with—a prospect

that was thrilling and, to be honest, a little bit overwhelming.

My L-shaped house (below) has two types of exterior cladding: "corncrib" horizontal wood clapboards on one side and vertical board and batten on the other. I chose an opaque black stain for the clapboard. For the vertical segments, I used a special rust-finish paint that looks like Corten, a steel alloy designed to weather naturally. Inspired by old vernacular utilitarian buildings but aware that the house was a simple modern structure with plenty of glass, I was going for the look and feel of an old barn/rusted shipping container/modernist Le Corbusier mash-up. I wanted the house to have weight, to hug the ground in the middle of the field filled with tall wild grasses.

Low and boxy, with many sets of sliding glass doors, the house opens to the outside in every direction. The interior is architecturally straightforward and without much ornamentation. The interior has been bright white, but over the past two years I have played with adding more color to the rooms. The guest bedroom now has a wall mural. The entrance (which doubles as a mudroom and an office) currently has a single coffee-brown wall. Meanwhile, the living room got a wall of mauve, which serves as a backdrop for a series of botanical prints.

Scarcely a weekend goes by without my taking brush and paint to something. I especially love to experiment with color outdoors. I often shop in the woodpile for small logs that I can turn into side tables; I give them drippy caps of tarlike black (glossy oil paint) both to seal the surface and to make them seem more interesting. I raise bees and paint the standard white beehives green so that they will better recede into the landscape. If my farm implements don't come in my favorite shade of John Deere green, I repaint them, as I did the disk harrow (for tilling soil) and York rake (for dragging over gravel to repair dirt roads), which arrived in a disappointing dull ochre. Using brightly colored porch and deck enamel in shades like hot pink, I even transformed a set of brown wicker outdoor chairs from Ikea. Against the dark stain of the house, they are now as brilliant and welcoming as a bed of poppies.

Left: My modern house has almost no trim to speak of, so I've used blocks of color in several rooms to define space. I chose this pale coffee brown because I liked how it looked behind the bookcase and coat racks. You see this wall from the dining table, which provides a nice sight line too.

Above: I love old prints, and these botanicals thrilled me with their almost sinister plant forms and exotic rich colors. I really struggled to find the right color for the wall behind them. At first I was convinced it should be indigo, but after I tested a few deep blues I realized that it was going to be too heavy in the small, bright room. Finally I landed on a color that feels like it emanates from the prints, a smoky mauvish-lavender.

Above: Looking at a book of Audubon bird prints inspired me to create a mural for the guest room. Noticing the landscapes behind the owls and egrets, I decided to paint just a background. Instead of birds in the foreground I hung art, three of my own works and one by a favorite professor. My guests love staying in this previously unremarkable room.

Top and above: The siding of my shed and a large section of my house are stained opaque matte black. I love the dark architecture against the lush fields in the summer and the snowy hills in the winter. To add a focal point to the shed, I painted its window frames a vibrant grass green in high-gloss oil

Above right: Even if I could afford to buy lots of fancy outdoor furniture, I know I'd still prefer to scour flea markets, junk shops, salvage yards, and tag sales for interesting, paintable stuff. I love how the 1950s tubular iron side table I found at a yard sale and painted glossy orange looks in front of the house's rusted steel siding.

Right: Hot pink is another color you rarely find on outdoor furniture, but I like the way it provides punch, just like bright flowers. A coat of pink and forest-green paint gave a totally new identity to a wicker chair from Ikea.

My Studio

The walls of my Manhattan studio are a pure white, for good reason. I need to see color clearly while I work and can't have the color of the walls influencing the way I perceive color samples and paint chips. I do have the advantage of being able to assess colors in varied light conditions, thanks to ample windows and a large north-facing skylight. In my white envelope of a studio, I've made

countless paint samples, tested colors and new materials, arranged and rearranged an endless array of flotsam and jetsam I find inspiring, and taken a brush to all kinds of inanimate objects, from prints and blocks to rocks and sticks.

Above left: One of many random collections of things found in my studio. I constantly add to and move around my seemingly endless supply of small objects.

Left: The brick walls have many layers of paint. It's hard for me to imagine this space in anything other than white, but it was once dark brown! As soon as I got the key to the loft I started painting everything white.

Above: Sample boards of my Essential Palette paint range hang on the studio wall, and there are layouts for this book on the canvas-covered work table.

Left: My supply and sink room is painted top to bottom in glossy white oil paint that has withstood years of use.

A New York State Farmhouse

Jeffrey Stark, Lisa Lancaster, and I first started talking about colors for their upstate farm in Dutchess County, New York, while studying their building plans in my studio. At that point in construction, the main farmhouse had only its foundation. The smaller building, referred to as the garage apartment, was already built and in need of paint—inside and out. As we discussed the project,

I learned of my clients' love of the Lake District in England, Shaker architecture, Dutch barns, agriculture, music, and art—all pieces of the puzzle that would influence their palette.

I was interested in how the two buildings were sited on a gently sloping hill with extraordinary, timeless views of silos and rolling fields that had been farmed for three hundred years. The main house was inspired by old Dutch barns still standing in nearby fields. It featured a silolike

structure that connected to the north face of the house. The windows at the top of the silo took in a panorama of the Berkshire and Taconic Mountains. Likewise, you could see the house from some distance if you were across the valley. I felt that the main house should not stand out but rather lie low on the hillside, like an unassuming old homestead. This ran counter to Jeff's initial thoughts of a classic red barn. For me the red would be too forceful, too visible from a distance, and potentially a cliché. Moreover, I didn't think we should or could compete with a cherished maple, transplanted from their former house on Long Island, that turned brilliant crimson in the fall.

Both buildings ended up being clad in siding from a reclaimed barn, which needed to be stained or painted. I suggested the main house be stained a weathered gray, with the trim painted deep gunmetal to give the new building a kind of handsome gravitas. The gray-on-gray combination did what I expected—it quieted the new house down, letting it settle into the hillside as if it had seen decades pass. Because the smaller structure looked like a more utilitarian outbuilding, I felt this would be the place to employ red, but a toned-down, aged red. For trim, I chose a warm white that wasn't glaring in the bright sun. It was important to both my clients and me that the two buildings form a harmonious compound in keeping with the spirit of the region.

Opposite: The garage and house frame a view. We had fun using classic barn red with white trim boards to make the garage relate to the neighboring farms.

Top: The western face of the house at sunset in late June.

Above left: The front of the main house in fall. The reclaimed barn wood siding with its gray stain makes the new house look as if it's been there for a long time. The gray stain was inspired by the colors of the stones in the retaining walls that flank the house.

Above right: The southern face of the house catches the crisp, bright sunlight of a fall day in the Hudson Valley. The red leaves of the Japanese maple were great inspiration for the garage barn.

A House in Beverly Hills

Several years ago I began work on a house in Southern California. The occupant was a single man in his late twenties. When I first saw the rambling manse of bubble-gum-pink stucco, I thought, "No way; he cannot be living in this Zsa Zsa Gabor of a house." At first we focused on the interiors of the late 1920s building. Spending time at the house helped me understand the way it sat, perched on

a steep grade, and how the trees clung to the hill sloping away below it. The landscaping literally climbed right up the walls. It became clear that using green on the exterior would serve dual purposes: it would help the house blend in with its landscape and it would also resonate with my client's temperament and his desire for privacy. I walked the grounds with my color decks, looking at various greens next to trees and plants, and chose several colors to test. The California sun made it difficult to work at midday—by noon it became impossible to see without sunglasses—so I set out early, in the even light of the shade, to look at colors. We settled on a eucalyptus hue. The house was radically transformed by its new coat. It looked indigenous, a bit sly, even a touch chic. I couldn't help but feel that the house itself was relieved to have shed its slightly embarrassing show-off pink.

Left: The stucco house in its original pink state—a color perfect for some inhabitants but not my client. The lush gardens were the inspiration for the greens that we tested. Since my client wanted a more "under the radar" house, I looked for colors that would embed the building in the landscape, reducing its prominence.

Left: The house took on a more natural feeling and looked quieter in its new green coat. No longer the "bright pink house on the hill," a description that made it easy for visitors to find, the sedate, almost hidden green house became the hideaway my client desired.

145

A Connecticut Colonial

A client's Georgian Revival house in Litchfield, Connecticut, is typical of the Colonial homes in this area, which is filled with classic American houses. This one was symmetrical and boxy, with a flat and modest face. Lawn circled the house and gave way to stone walls and woods. The owner said he wanted the house to be neither too bright nor too dark, cheerful but not silly. And he wanted

to use one predominant color on all of the various buildings on his seventy-five-acre property. He ruled out green as well as the existing gray. I showed him a few warm tans and deep creams from a historical color chart. "Bravo! That's the right direction," he told me. With that encouragement, I tested a range of colors directly on the property's main house, which is something I always do, especially when dealing with a clapboard exterior. (For more on testing exterior colors, see page 33.) Clapboards create shadows

that alter color in unexpected ways. Since my client had already settled on an almost-black green for the shutters, I propped a freestanding shutter against my color tests to see how different combinations worked.

Once the color scheme was finalized, a team of painters set about carefully preparing the wooden house for paint. Such preparation is particularly important in an environment that is subject to moisture and extreme temperature shifts. Damp or rotting boards were removed and replaced. We scraped away any loose, chipped, or flaking paint. The entire exterior was then washed with TSP (trisodium phosphate), a cleaning agent composed of soda ash and phosphoric acid that removes mildew and dirt. Only then was the house thoroughly primed and painted.

If you decide to become the steward of an old wooden home, be prepared for a lifelong commitment to its upkeep. Professional preparation and high-quality paint will reduce your burden considerably. I recommend monitoring the exterior of a wooden house annually for mildew, cracks, and small paint defects. Address these issues immediately to avoid moisture damage to your home. The longevity of the paint will vary, depending on the manufacturer; look at the warranty when you are deciding which paint to use.

Above: For the color testing process, I had the painter prime the lower part of the house on several sides so we could see large areas of prospective colors in varying exposures and times of day. I know we liked the blackish-green shutter color, so I had one painted to use during the color testing phase. It was helpful to see the house colors with the shutter when we looked at our options.

Left: Ultimately we chose the color on the right, a khaki that felt historically accurate, looked great with the shutter color, and pleased my client. Once the colors were chosen, the painters prepped and primed the entire house before applying the finish coats.

Opposite: The house in its finished state. With its clapboards restored, shutters hung, and a new coat of paint, the house looks handsome and renewed.

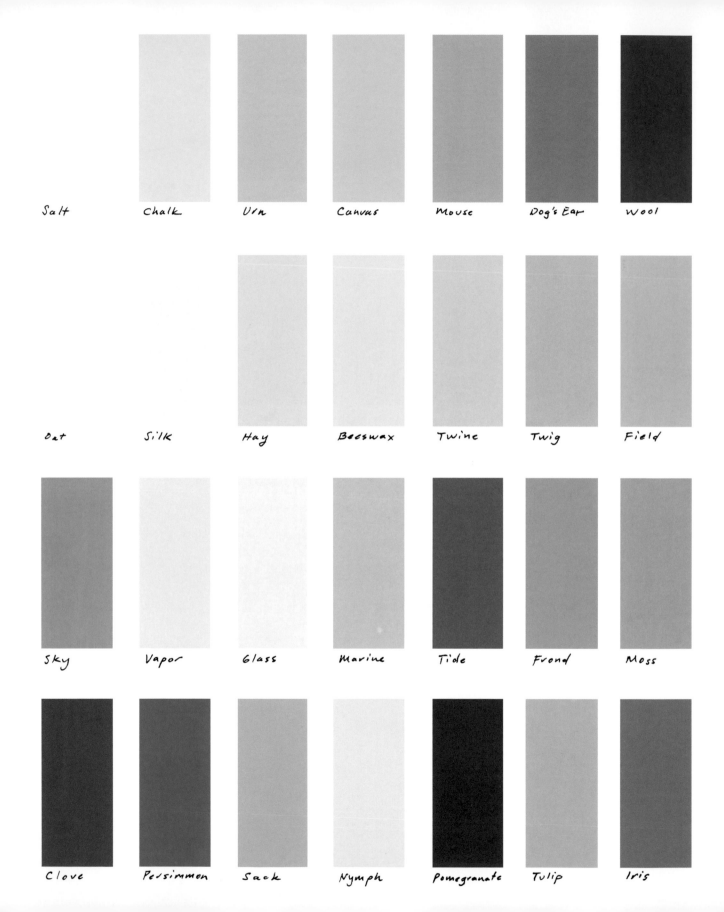

Salt   Chalk   Urn   Canvas   Mouse   Dog's Ear   Wool

Oat   Silk   Hay   Beeswax   Twine   Twig   Field

Sky   Vapor   Glass   Marine   Tide   Frond   Moss

Clove   Persimmon   Sack   Nymph   Pomegranate   Tulip   Iris

6

TWENTY-EIGHT COLORS THAT WORK

Designing a paint line is about looking at colors and seeing how they relate as a group. I've designed paint collections for several companies. The hardest part is figuring out what grouping of colors will not only work well together but also tell a kind of story. Martha Stewart's first paint range, Araucana Colors, was hatched from a basket of pastel-colored eggs that she gave me for inspiration. Named for the

breed of chickens that laid the eggs, the collection consisted of just twenty-four colors—mostly blues, greens, creams, and browns. Though that was a very limited range for a paint collection at the time, it was hugely successful. Because the edited collection was harmonious from the start, decision making was much easier. I realized then that many people were happy to have fewer rather than more colors from which to choose. Martha's next paint range, Everyday Colors, was, at 256 colors, far larger. For inspiration, she offered me personal objects whose colors she loved, from old English ironstone to sweaters. Deriving paint colors from favorite possessions is often what I do for my clients today—and what you too can do when developing your own color schemes.

I worked my way through thousands of hues for my own collection, Eve Ashcraft Color: The Essential Palette, manufactured by Fine Paints of Europe. I wanted to use what I've come to know from working with color for thirty years, distilled into a limited collection of twenty-eight colors that all play well together. Though my palette covers the full spectrum, it espouses the old-fashioned idea that one or two good versions of a color will do fine. The idea was to create a palette that is both inspiring and easy, a user-friendly helping hand for achieving the beautiful rooms you desire.

SALT

COLOR NO. 1
Salt

COLOR PROFILE
The whitest white, with the subtlest of undertones that help it stay neutral—neither too warm nor too cool.

COLORS INSIDE THE COLOR
Tiny amounts of yellow, green, and red pigments.

BEST USES
The workhorse white, all-purpose and trustworthy, to be used everywhere, on every surface.

EXTERIOR RECOMMENDATIONS
Use for a crisp trim color on a traditional house. Pair with Dog's Ear for the house body color for a classic New England look.

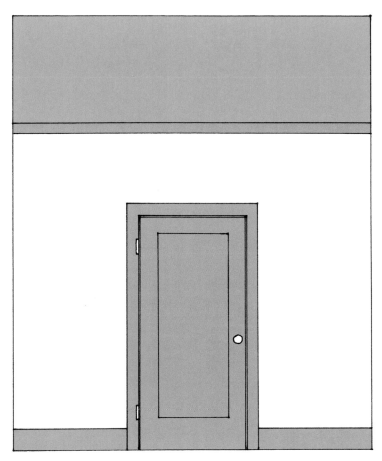

A Daring Combination

WALLS: Salt TRIM: Twig CEILING: Field

Color Options for Adjacent Rooms

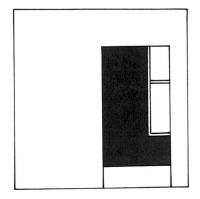

BOLD: Clove

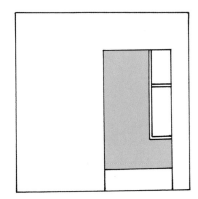

MIDTONE: Twine

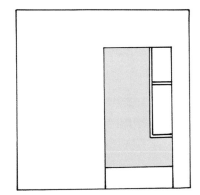

LIGHT: Nymph

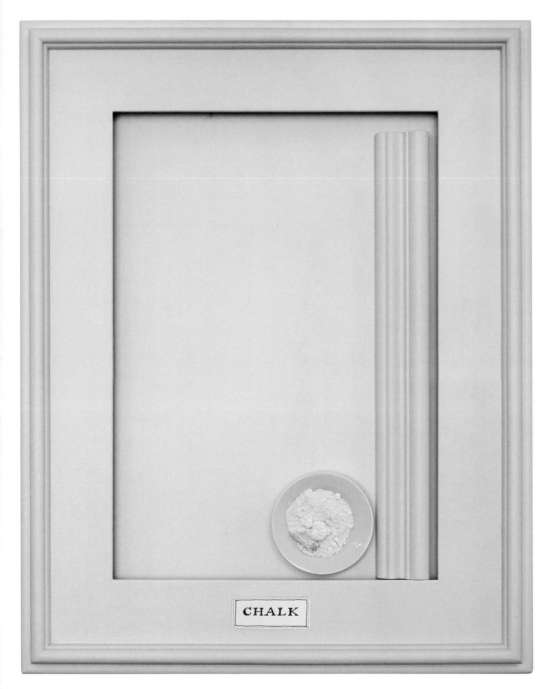

CHALK

Chalk

COLOR PROFILE
A gray white, a bit cooler and quieter than Salt.

COLORS INSIDE THE COLOR
Looks like white with a pinch of black, but also contains small amounts of green and yellow.

BEST USES
Another all-purpose color. Suits trim in older houses; makes a ceiling pale and calm.

EXTERIOR RECOMMENDATIONS
For an all-white house, use Chalk for the body and Salt for the trim. For a pale yellow house, use Twine for the body and Chalk for the trim.

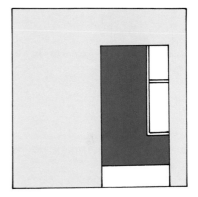

Color Options for Adjacent Rooms

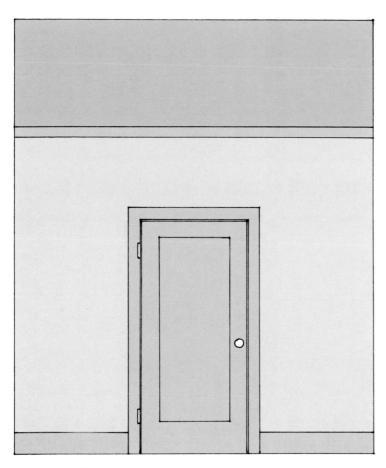

A Lovely Combination
WALLS: Chalk · TRIM: Twine · CEILING: Urn

BOLD: Persimmon

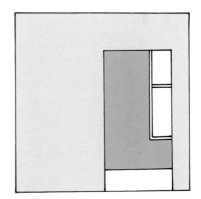

MIDTONE: Tulip

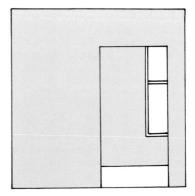

LIGHT: Beeswax

URN

COLOR NO. 3

Urn

COLOR PROFILE
A pale, quiet medium gray.

COLORS INSIDE THE COLOR
A surprising shot of yellow along with black, for a seemingly simple gray.

BEST USES
A shadowy color to be used where a calm attitude is desired. Works well in both classical and modern environments.

EXTERIOR RECOMMENDATIONS
Use as the body color, with Salt or Wool as the trim, for a pale gray look.

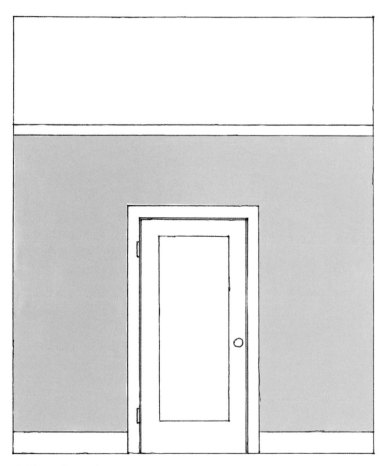

A Zen Combination
WALLS: Urn · **TRIM:** Oat · **CEILING:** Salt

Color Options for Adjacent Rooms

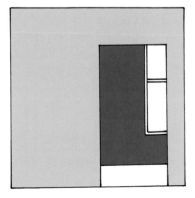

BOLD: Wool

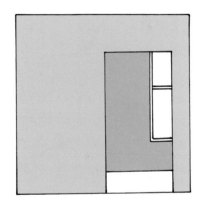

MIDTONE: Sky

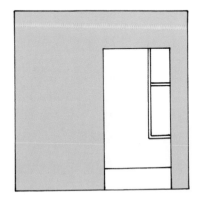

LIGHT: Silk

CANVAS

Canvas

COLOR PROFILE
My answer to beige;
a warm neutral to use
anywhere.

COLORS INSIDE THE COLOR
Yellow and red oxides,
plus a shot of black.

BEST USES
As a neutral backdrop in
any room. Works well with
natural materials (wood,
stone, sea grass) in subtle
shades.

EXTERIOR RECOMMENDATIONS
On a stone house, use for
a coordinating trim. On a
stucco house, use for the
body color with Oat or
Moss for the trim.

A Seaside Combination
WALLS: Canvas · TRIM: Salt · CEILING: Glass

Color Options for Adjacent Rooms

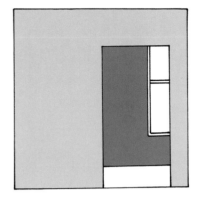

BOLD: Iris

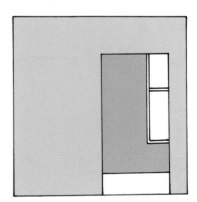

MIDTONE: Sack

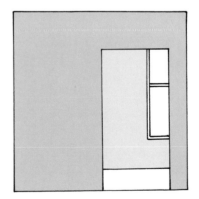

LIGHT: Vapor

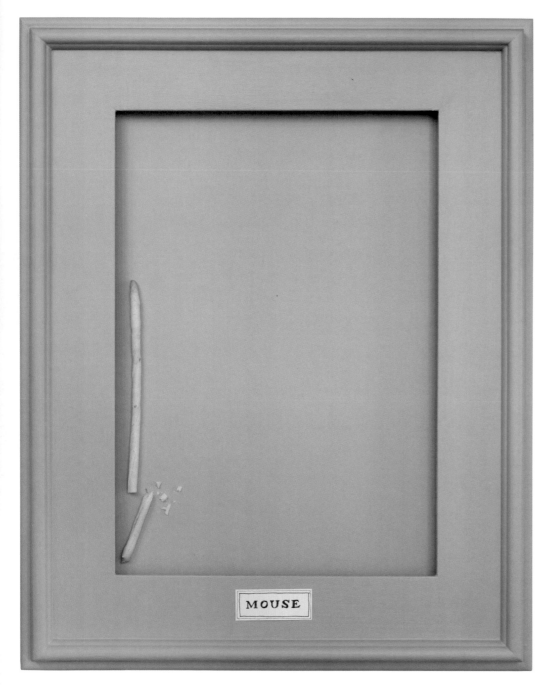

MOUSE

Mouse

COLOR PROFILE

A soft, warm gray.

COLORS INSIDE THE COLOR

Yellow and red oxides, plus a shot of black—like Canvas, but in different quantities.

BEST USES

As a deeper neutral backdrop in any room. Bright colors are nicely balanced with Mouse as a background. I like hanging art on this color.

EXTERIOR RECOMMENDATIONS

Use Mouse as the body and Hay as the trim for a cheerful gray house.

A Bold Combination

WALLS: Mouse • TRIM: Frond • CEILING: Beeswax

Color Options for Adjacent Rooms

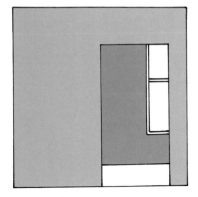

BOLD: Dog's Ear

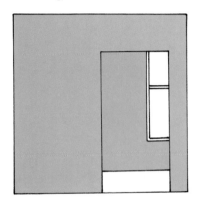

MIDTONE: Sky

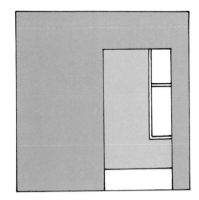

LIGHT: Urn

DOG'S EAR

Dog's Ear

COLOR PROFILE
A rich gray with a warm reddish undertone.

COLORS INSIDE THE COLOR
Yellow and red oxides, plus a shot of black; contains a greater amount of red than Mouse.

BEST USES
For a warm and cozy night-time room. Or as a deep, neutral trim and cabinet color.

EXTERIOR RECOMMENDATIONS
Makes a classic and hand-some body color. For trim try Beeswax or Moss.

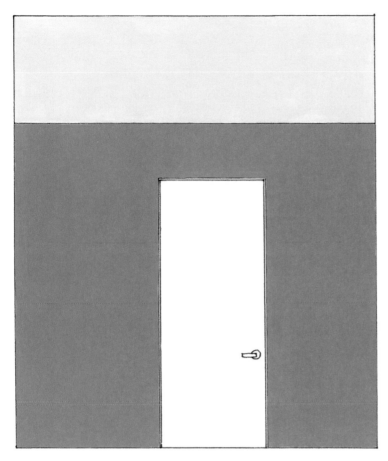

A Soothing Combination

WALLS: Dog's Ear · TRIM: Oat · CEILING: Glass

Color Options for Adjacent Rooms

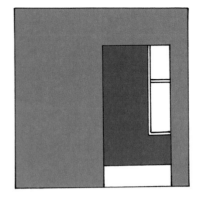

BOLD: Clove

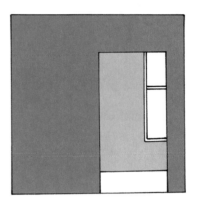

MIDTONE: Field

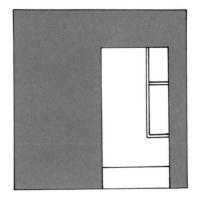

LIGHT: Salt

161

WOOL

COLOR NO. 7
Wool

COLOR PROFILE
A deep but soft gray,
like gunmetal.

COLORS INSIDE THE COLOR
Black, white, yellow,
and red oxides.

BEST USES
Lighter and softer than true
black, a little less severe but
still commanding.

EXTERIOR RECOMMENDATIONS
Use for trim on a house
painted Moss in a tradi-
tional setting. Or use for
the entire house for a
modern feel.

An Elegant Combination
WALLS: Wool • TRIM: Urn • CEILING: Salt

Color Options for Adjacent Rooms

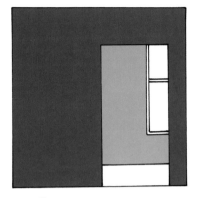

BOLD: Sky

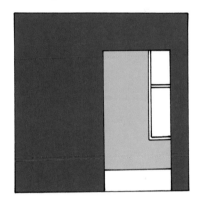

MIDTONE: Twig

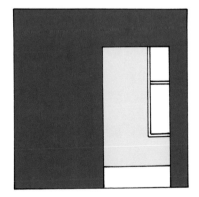

LIGHT: Nymph

OAT

Oat

COLOR PROFILE
A soft white, the warmer neighbor of Salt.

COLORS INSIDE THE COLOR
Yellow and green oxides.

BEST USES
Anywhere you want a soft but clean white; a beautiful trim color.

EXTERIOR RECOMMENDATIONS
Pair as a perfect, classic trim color with just about any body color. At the beach, try it with Marine.

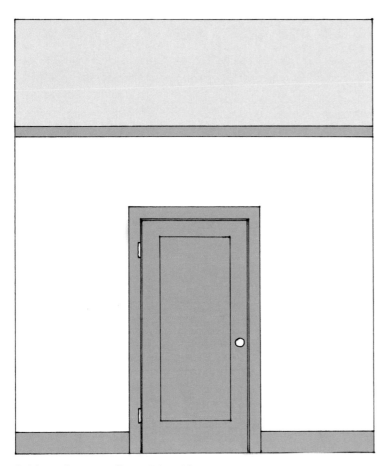

A Handsome Combination
WALLS: Oat · TRIM: Mouse · CEILING: Nymph

Color Options for Adjacent Rooms

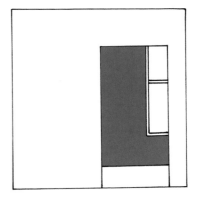

BOLD: Tide

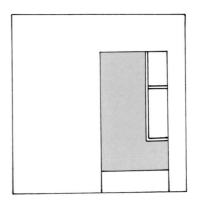

MIDTONE: Canvas

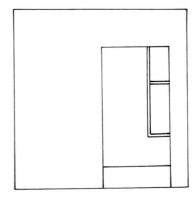

LIGHT: Silk

SILK

COLOR NO. 9

Silk

COLOR PROFILE

A pale yellow with a little heft to knock down the pastel sweetness associated with this color.

COLORS INSIDE THE COLOR

Green oxide, two types of yellow.

BEST USES

A pretty color made more handsome by pairing it with grays or sweeter by framing it with Salt. Perfect for a baby's room or any bedroom. Works well throughout the house.

EXTERIOR RECOMMENDATIONS

Use as the body color with Chalk as the trim, for something light and classic. Or pair with Dog's Ear trim for greater contrast.

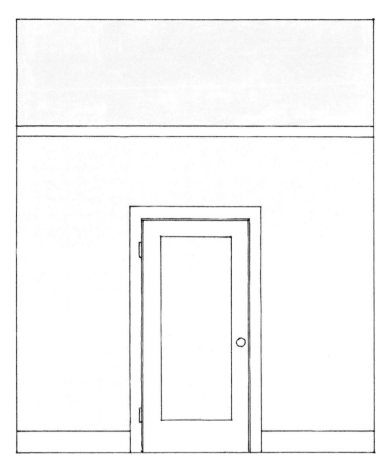

A Pretty Combination

WALLS: Silk · TRIM: Salt · CEILING: Nymph

Color Options for Adjacent Rooms

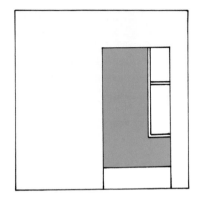

BOLD: Frond

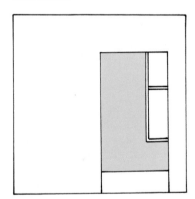

MIDTONE: Hay

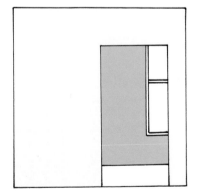

LIGHT: Urn

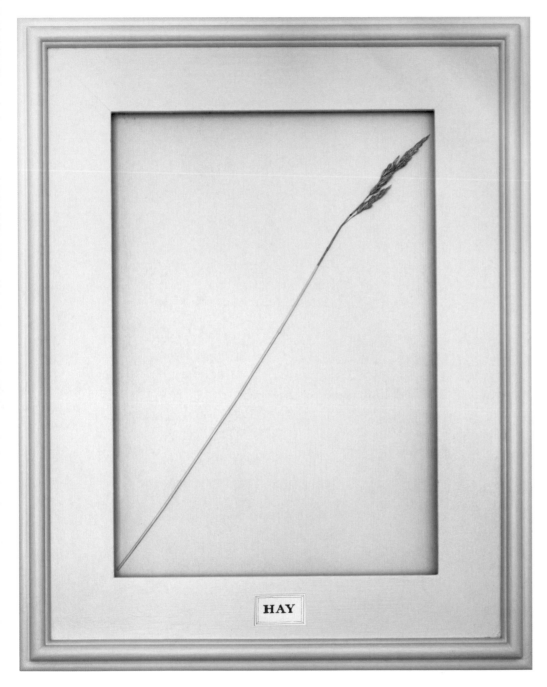

HAY

COLOR NO. 10

Hay

COLOR PROFILE

A medium, golden yellow.

COLORS INSIDE THE COLOR

Two types of yellow, green oxide.

BEST USES

Reminds me of France. A lovely kitchen color; also good in the living room.

EXTERIOR RECOMMENDATIONS

Use as the shutter color on a house painted Dog's Ear. Or as the body color with Urn for the trim.

A Daring Combination

WALLS: Hay • **TRIM:** Pomegranate • **CEILING:** Beeswax

Color Options for Adjacent Rooms

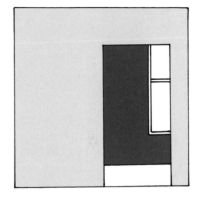

BOLD: Clove

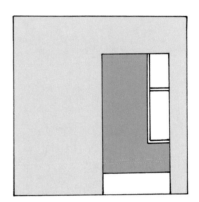

MIDTONE: Moss

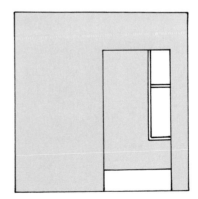

LIGHT: Chalk

BEESWAX

Beeswax

COLOR PROFILE

A pale, gray yellow.

COLORS INSIDE THE COLOR

Two types of yellow plus black.

BEST USES

A warm neutral that's a bit unexpected. Works well everywhere. Use in place of run-of-the-mill off-whites.

EXTERIOR RECOMMENDATIONS

Use as a body color with Dog's Ear trim for a quiet, classic look.

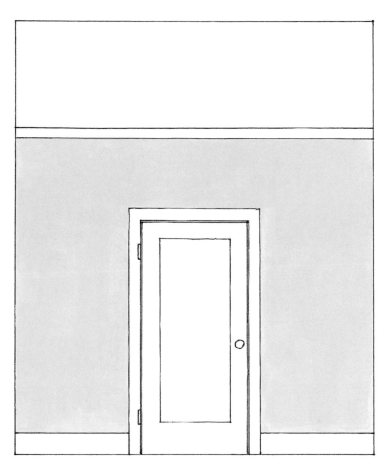

A Quiet Combination

WALLS: Beeswax • TRIM: Oat • CEILING: Salt

Color Options for Adjacent Rooms

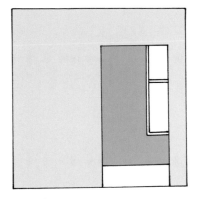

BOLD: Sky

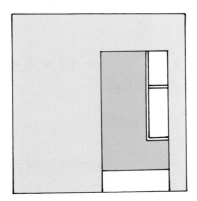

MIDTONE: Marine

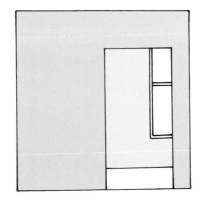

LIGHT: Glass

TWINE

Twine

COLOR PROFILE
A deep, warm neutral.

COLORS INSIDE THE COLOR
Two types of yellow,
plus black.

BEST USES
Works well everywhere,
especially in older houses.

EXTERIOR RECOMMENDATIONS
Use as a body color with
Oat trim for a subtle
contrast.

A Classic Combination

WALLS: Twine • TRIM: Mouse • CEILING: Oat

Color Options for Adjacent Rooms

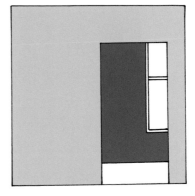

BOLD: Persimmon

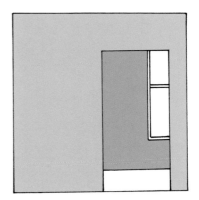

MIDTONE: Sack

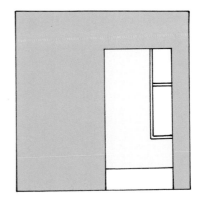

LIGHT: Silk

TWIG

Twig

COLOR PROFILE

A warm putty color.

COLORS INSIDE THE COLOR

Two types of yellow,
plus black.

BEST USES

A great color for historical
houses; works beautifully
as a backdrop for antique
furniture. Also a perfect
deep neutral to use with
organic and natural design
elements like raw linen
and bleached or limed oak
furniture.

EXTERIOR RECOMMENDATIONS

Use for trim with Oat as a
body color for a crisply
tailored white house.

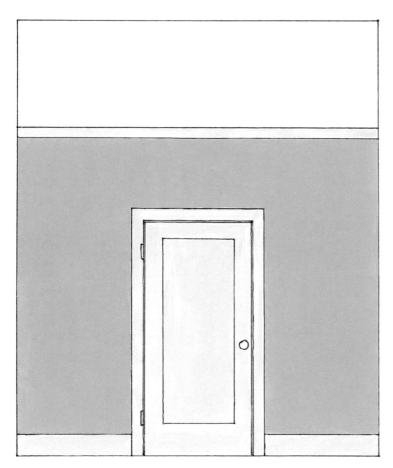

A Peaceful Combination
WALLS: Twig · TRIM: Chalk · CEILING: Oat

Color Options for Adjacent Rooms

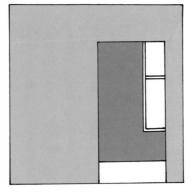

BOLD: Dog's Ear

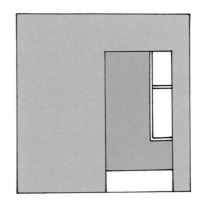

MIDTONE: Sack

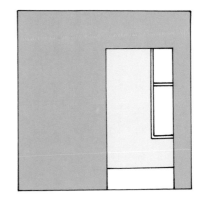

LIGHT: Glass

FIELD

COLOR NO. 14
Field

COLOR PROFILE
A lively middle green.

COLORS INSIDE THE COLOR
Full of surprises: yellow, orange, red, and blue.

BEST USES
A cheerful and pleasing color, good for a guest room or a dining room, or inside kitchen cabinets.

EXTERIOR RECOMMENDATIONS
Makes a beautiful porch ceiling color. Also try it in a potting shed or for outdoor furniture.

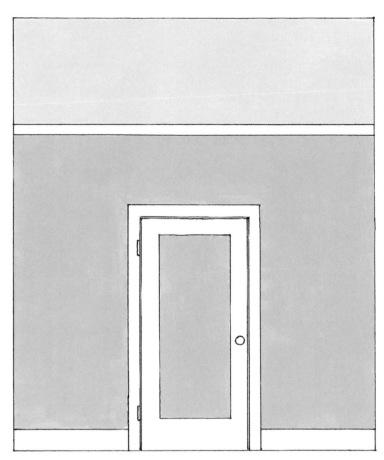

A Fresh Combination

WALLS: Field · TRIM: Salt · CEILING: Vapor

Color Options for Adjacent Rooms

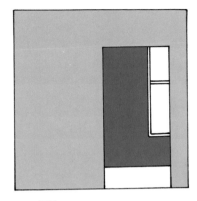

BOLD: Tide

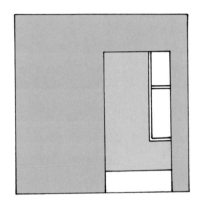

MIDTONE: Twine

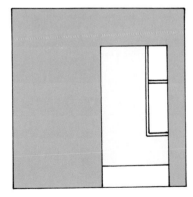

LIGHT: Silk

COLOR NO. 15

Sky

COLOR PROFILE
A clear, slightly periwinkle blue.

COLORS INSIDE THE COLOR
Violet, blue, and a pinch of black.

BEST USES
An uplifting color, good for kids' rooms, the home office, and the kitchen. Also works well inside cabinets and bookcases.

EXTERIOR RECOMMENDATIONS
Use for a porch ceiling or the front door of a beach house. Also great for outdoor furniture.

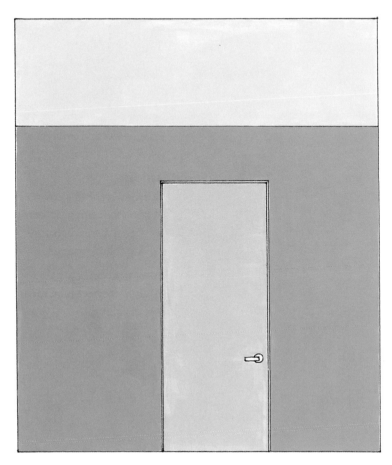

A Beachy Combination
WALLS: Sky · TRIM: Urn · CEILING: Vapor

Color Options for Adjacent Rooms

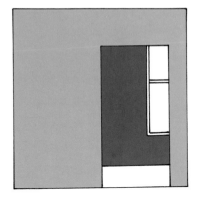

BOLD: Clove

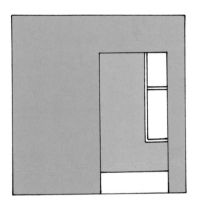

MIDTONE: Mouse

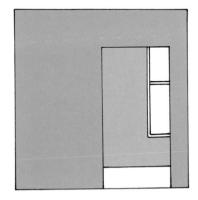

LIGHT: Tulip

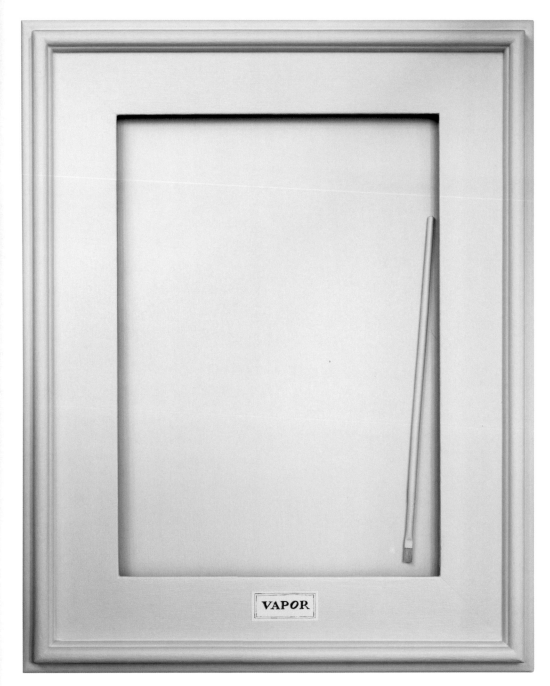

COLOR NO. 16

Vapor

COLOR PROFILE

A very pale blue.

COLORS INSIDE THE COLOR

Blue-violet and two types
of green.

BEST USES

A lovely bathroom color.
Perfect for ceilings. Works
well anywhere a light, uplifting color is wanted.

EXTERIOR RECOMMENDATIONS

Makes a perfect color for a
porch ceiling.

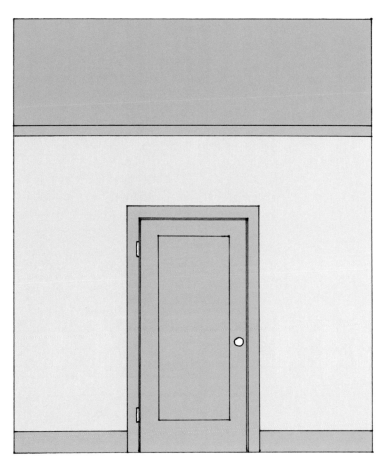

An Elegant Combination
WALLS: Vapor • TRIM: Urn • CEILING: Tulip

Color Options for Adjacent Rooms

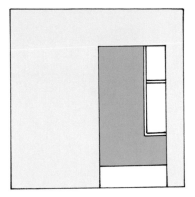

BOLD: Sky

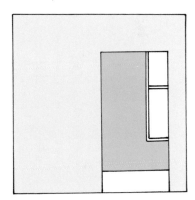

MIDTONE: Marine

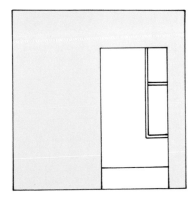

LIGHT: Oat

GLASS

Glass

COLOR PROFILE
A very pale greenish blue.

COLORS INSIDE THE COLOR
Surprisingly, green *and* red!

BEST USES
For a soft bedroom, bathrooms, and ceilings.

EXTERIOR RECOMMENDATIONS
Use as a great alternative to white for metal poolside furniture.

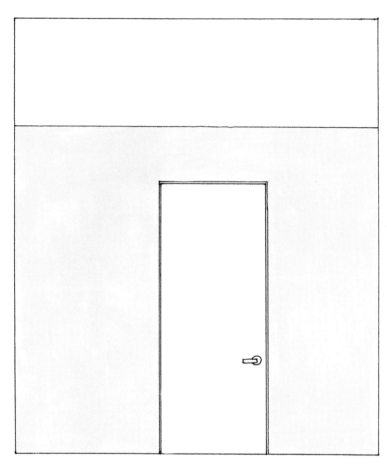

A Crisp Combination

WALLS: Glass · **TRIM:** Oat · **CEILING:** Salt

Color Options for Adjacent Rooms

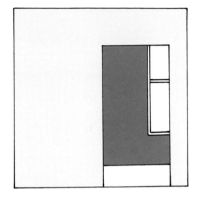

BOLD: Iris

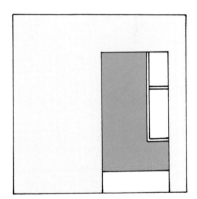

MIDTONE: Moss

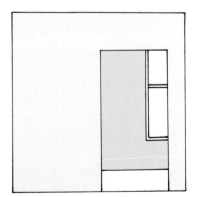

LIGHT: Chalk

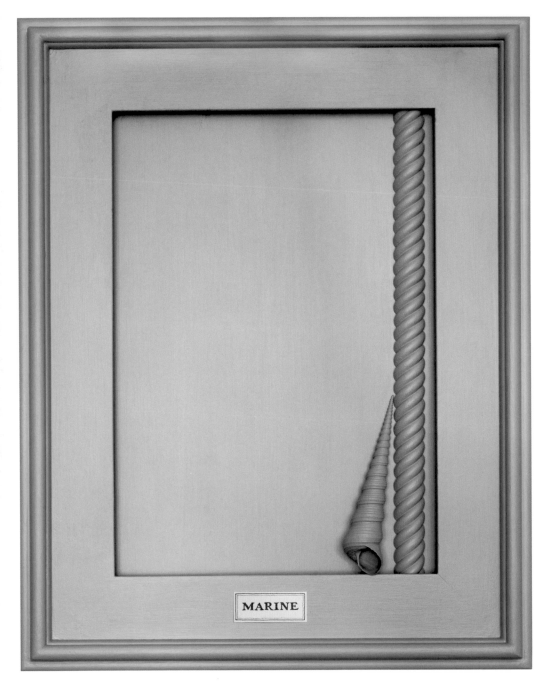

MARINE

Marine

COLOR PROFILE
A greenish blue.

COLORS INSIDE THE COLOR
Blue, yellow, and black.

BEST USES
Goes from the dining room to the playroom. Great for older houses.

EXTERIOR RECOMMENDATIONS
Use for a body color with Salt or Wool trim. An excellent shutter color on a white or gray house.

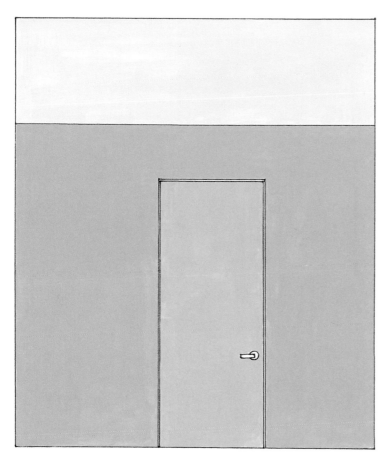

A Playful Combination
WALLS: Marine · TRIM: Field · CEILING: Glass

Color Options for Adjacent Rooms

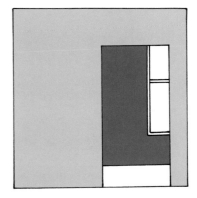

BOLD: Tide

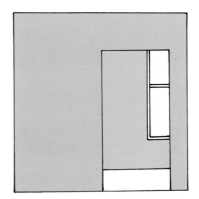

MIDTONE: Twine

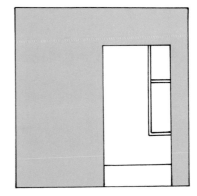

LIGHT: Oat

TIDE

Tide

COLOR PROFILE
A deep greenish-blue teal.

COLORS INSIDE THE COLOR
White, yellow, blue, and black.

BEST USES
A dignified color well suited to dining and living rooms, libraries, and bedrooms.

EXTERIOR RECOMMENDATIONS
Use as the body color with Twig or Canvas trim. A beautiful front door color.

A Handsome Combination
WALLS: Tide • TRIM: Sack • CEILING: Oat

Color Options for Adjacent Rooms

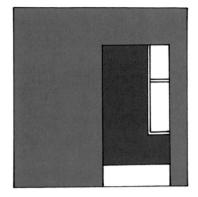

BOLD: Pomegranate

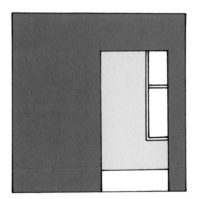

MIDTONE: Hay

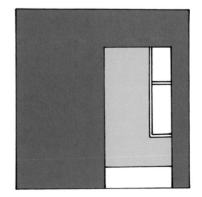

LIGHT: Urn

FROND

COLOR NO. 20
Frond

COLOR PROFILE
A fresh, leafy green.

COLORS INSIDE THE COLOR
White, green, two types
of yellow.

BEST USES
A cheerful color that's great
for kids' rooms, hallways,
sunporches—anywhere you
need a high note.

EXTERIOR RECOMMENDATIONS
Great for outdoor furniture,
a porch floor, or a glossy
front door.

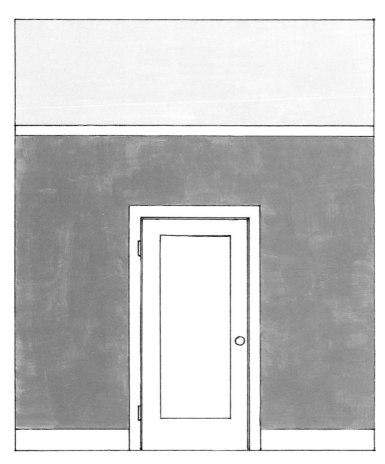

A Lively Combination

WALLS: Frond · TRIM: Salt · CEILING: Glass

Color Options for Adjacent Rooms

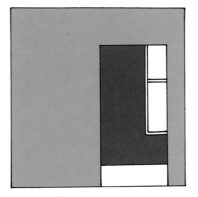

BOLD: Wool

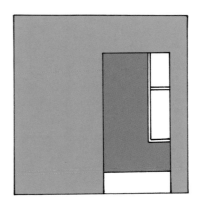

MIDTONE: Dog's Ear

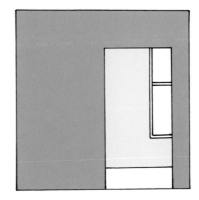

LIGHT: Vapor

MOSS

Moss

COLOR PROFILE
A sage green.

COLORS INSIDE THE COLOR
Yellow, orange, and blue.

BEST USES
A classic color, inside and out. Good for a dining room or bedroom.

EXTERIOR RECOMMENDATIONS
Makes a nice body color, with Oat or Dog's Ear for the trim. Also great for shutters on a white house.

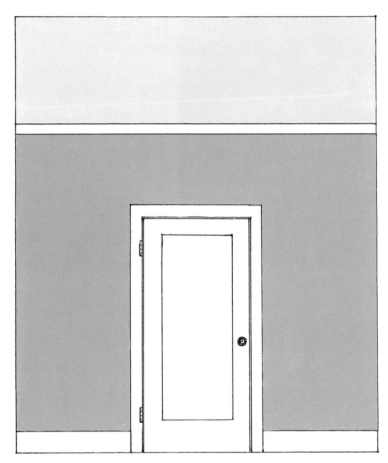

An Attractive Combination

WALLS: Moss · TRIM: Salt · CEILING: Nymph

Color Options for Adjacent Rooms

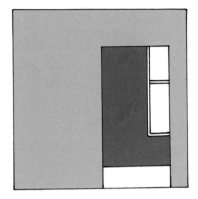

BOLD: Clove

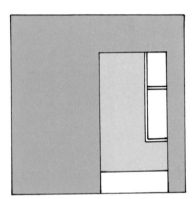

MIDTONE: Twine

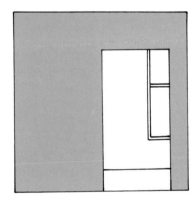

LIGHT: Silk

CLOVE

Clove

COLOR PROFILE

A warm chocolate brown.

COLORS INSIDE THE COLOR

Yellow, red, black, and white.

BEST USES

A handsome brown that works beautifully in a living room, dining room, or bedroom.

EXTERIOR RECOMMENDATIONS

For a handsome Colonial scheme, use for the body *and* the trim, with glossy Persimmon on the front door.

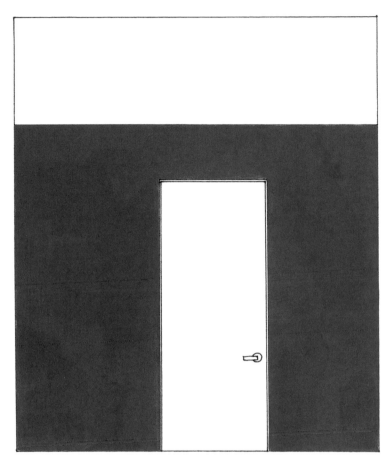

An Elegant Combination

WALLS: Clove • TRIM: Salt • CEILING: Oat

Color Options for Adjacent Rooms

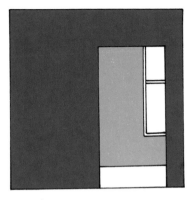

BOLD: Sky

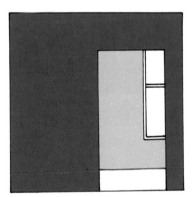

MIDTONE: Field

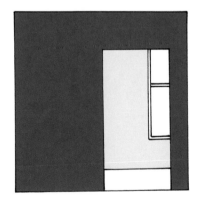

LIGHT: Beeswax

PERSIMMON

Persimmon

COLOR PROFILE

A burnt orange.

COLORS INSIDE THE COLOR

White, orange, yellow, and red.

BEST USES

For an entryway, a powder room, or anywhere you want a bold color.

EXTERIOR RECOMMENDATIONS

Looks great on the front door in a glossy finish.

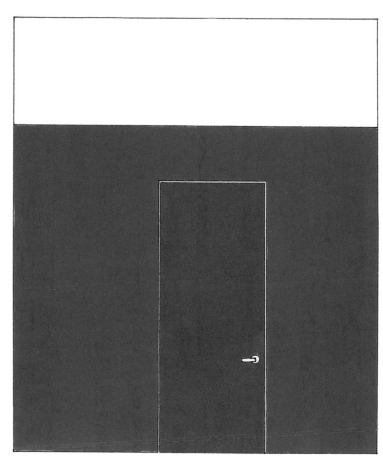

A Modern Combination

WALLS: Persimmon · TRIM: Wool · CEILING: Salt

Color Options for Adjacent Rooms

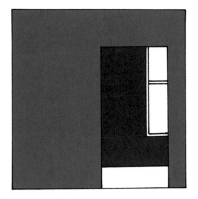

BOLD: Pomegranate

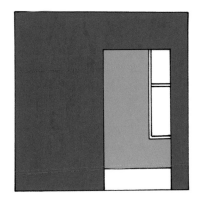

MIDTONE: Moss

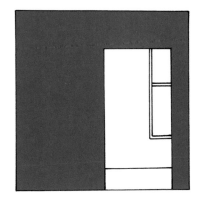

LIGHT: Oat

SACK

COLOR NO. 24

Sack

COLOR PROFILE
A warm tan.

COLORS INSIDE THE COLOR
Yellow, red, and black.

BEST USES
An unassuming color, great for warming up a neutral space or offsetting art and colorful furnishings.

EXTERIOR RECOMMENDATIONS
Use as a body color with Oat for trim and Wool for the shutters.

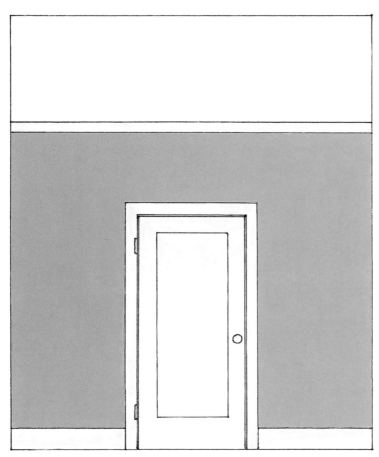

A Subtle Combination

WALLS: Sack · TRIM: Beeswax · CEILING: Oat

Color Options for Adjacent Rooms

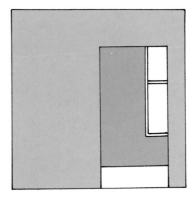

BOLD: Frond

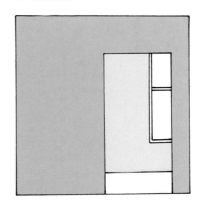

MIDTONE: Hay

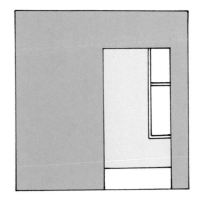

LIGHT: Chalk

Nymph

COLOR PROFILE
A warm pale pink.

COLORS INSIDE THE COLOR
Yellow and red.

BEST USES
Perfect for bedrooms or bathrooms and for ceilings.

EXTERIOR RECOMMENDATIONS
Works beautifully as a body color when paired with deeper colors like Wool or Clove for trim.

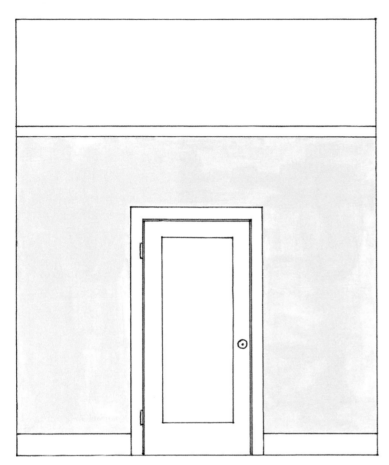

A Pretty Combination
WALLS: Nymph • **TRIM:** Oat • **CEILING:** Salt

Color Options for Adjacent Rooms

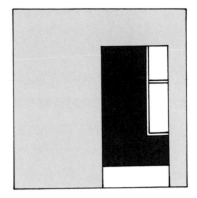

BOLD: Pomegranate

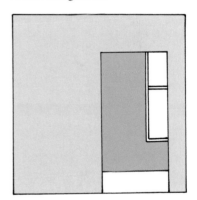

MIDTONE: Twig

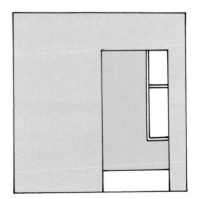

LIGHT: Chalk

POMEGRANATE

Pomegranate

COLOR PROFILE

A burgundy red.

COLORS INSIDE THE COLOR

Violet, yellow, and red.

BEST USES

Makes a bold statement. Great for entry halls, powder rooms, dining rooms, and densely decorated spaces.

EXTERIOR RECOMMENDATIONS

A great accent color; use on a front door, shutters, or window boxes.

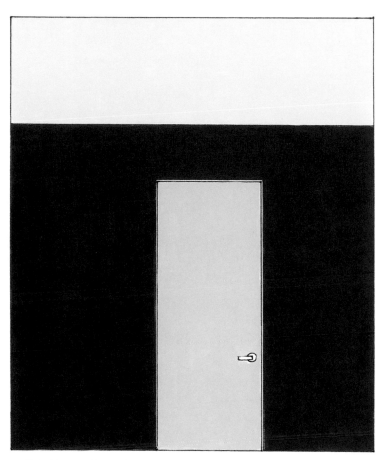

A Distinct Combination

WALLS: Pomegranate · TRIM: Canvas · CEILING: Glass

Color Options for Adjacent Rooms

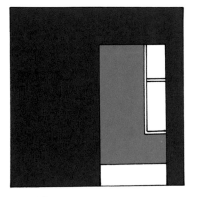

BOLD: Iris

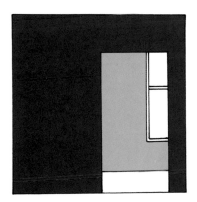

MIDTONE: Sack

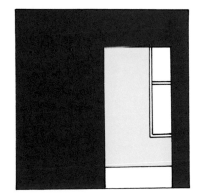

LIGHT: Vapor

TULIP

Tulip

COLOR PROFILE

A pale lavender.

COLORS INSIDE THE COLOR

Blue-violet, red, and black.

BEST USES

A pretty color that is great for bedrooms. A good balance for more masculine colors like Clove or Wool.

EXTERIOR RECOMMENDATIONS

More of an interior color, but works well for porch ceilings.

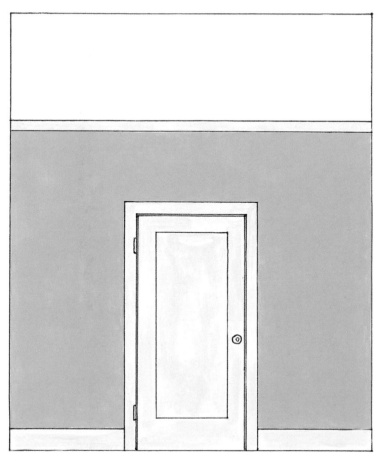

A Lovely Combination

WALLS: Tulip · TRIM: Chalk · CEILING: Salt

Color Options for Adjacent Rooms

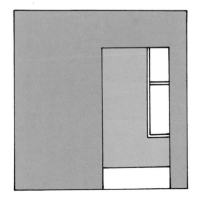

BOLD: Field

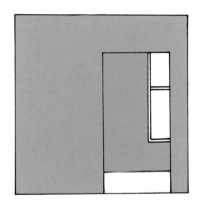

MIDTONE: Moss

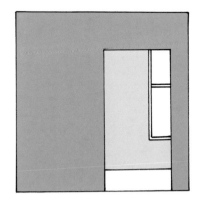

LIGHT: Chalk

IRIS

COLOR NO. 28
Iris

COLOR PROFILE
A midtone lavender-purple.

COLORS INSIDE THE COLOR
Two types of red and
blue-violet.

BEST USES
A bold backdrop for dark
furnishings.

EXTERIOR RECOMMENDATIONS
Works nicely for a garden
bench or café chairs.

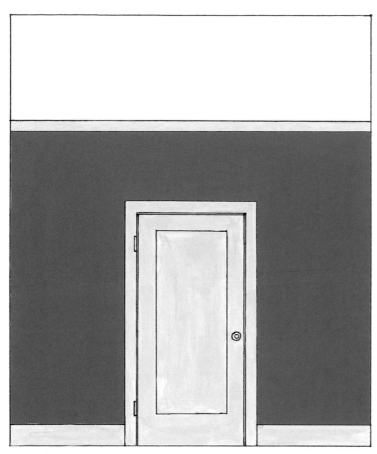

An Elegant Combination
WALLS: Iris • TRIM: Chalk • CEILING: Salt

Color Options for Adjacent Rooms

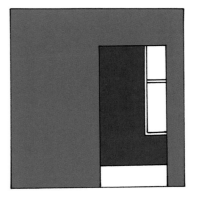

BOLD: Clove

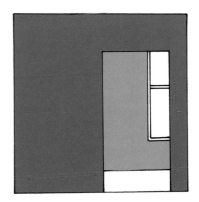

MIDTONE: Sack

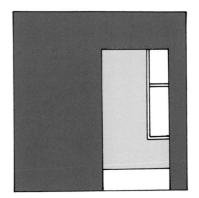

LIGHT: Beeswax

Ready, Set, Paint

Ready-made paint has been available for only the last 150 years, when machines were invented that could grind pigments fine enough to be suspended in binders and solvents. Before then, skilled tradesmen created paint from dry pigments, lead, and oil. In the late nineteenth century, advances in printing technology enabled paint companies to produce color cards and brochures, which were

distributed alongside pattern books for house components; for the first time, everyone had access, via catalogs, to mass-produced fixtures, materials, appliances, and paint. Homeowners suddenly had quandaries they had never before encountered, an embarrassment of riches. As early as 1885, Sherwin-Williams produced the book *What Color?* for their customers.

House paint has changed continually ever since it was first put into standardized production. Early paint often contained lead as a primary ingredient. Lead made paint durable, hard, and moisture resistant, while speeding up the drying time of the oil. Despite the health hazards of lead, especially to children, the substance wasn't banned in this country until 1978. Since then, the paint industry has invested in research and development that has led to many improvements in paint formulations. Today's paints are durable, colorfast, easy to work with, simple to clean up, and more ecologically friendly than ever before.

Paint is made from four basic ingredients—pigments, a binder or resin, solvent, and addi-

tives. Pigments vary in quantity and quality. More expensive paints generally have higher levels of pigment. The more pigment, the denser the paint, and the fewer coats needed to cover. In other words, good paint may cost more, but you'll need less of it. The binder or resin is the "glue" of paint. It sticks to the surface and forms a film that contains the pigments. Solvent is liquid that dilutes the binder—water in waterborne paints and mineral spirits or paint thinner in alkyd-based paints. Additives range from driers to mildew inhibitors and flow enhancers.

Many well-known, high-quality brands of paint are mass-produced. Recently smaller boutique paint brands have proliferated. It is worth investing in the highest quality paint you can afford: you get what you pay for. And what you want to pay for is lots of pigment and grade A ingredients. Look on the can or on the manufacturer's Web site for the percentage of solids per container (you want 45 percent or higher). But beware—some cheap paint will list a high solids percentage, but the content will be filler, not prime ingredients.

Paint: Questions and Answers

The following are a few of the most common questions I get about house paint.

Q **What is full spectrum paint, and do I need to buy it?**
A **There is a lot of talk about how paint with many pigments, often referred to as "full spectrum," is visually superior.** This is true to a point. You do want high-quality pigment in your paint, especially for coverage. But the other ingredients of house paint are utilitarian substances that do little to enhance any specific pigment combination. In my experience, the magic of paint color has more to do with light, environment, and a professional paint job than with the actual number of pigments in the paint itself.

Q **What is the difference between latex and oil paint? What type should I buy?**
A **Odd as it may seem, there is no latex in latex paint, nor is there oil in oil paint.** We continue to use these terms because they are familiar, but they no longer describe what's actually in the can. Water-soluble "latex" is now the predominant type of paint available. Waterborne house paints are made with acrylic or vinyl polymer resins. Paint that is 100 percent acrylic is durable, long lasting, and the best type of waterborne paint on the market today. "Oil" paint is made with alkyd resin, which is soluble with mineral spirits. Alkyd-based paints are still used for areas subject to heavy use, such as floors, doors, trims, and cabinets, but they are being phased out of the consumer market for environmental reasons.

The paint industry has made major progress in developing waterborne paints that can match the durability of alkyd-based paints. There are many pluses to working with high-quality waterborne paints. They are friendlier to the environment, have less odor, dry quickly, are easy to clean up, and form a breathable, flexible surface that, especially on exterior applications, is much longer lasting than oil paint. Oil paint dries to a hard shell that is susceptible to chipping and cracking when the painted surface expands and contracts as moisture or temperature changes. It also allows moisture caused by condensation to be trapped between the surface and the paint film, creating pockets where mildew can develop. Some contractors still swear by oil paint, but I think that view is outdated. If you have concerns about which paint is right for your project, I recommend visiting a few manufacturers' Web sites. You will find extensive information about which paints to select for various conditions and surfaces.

Q **Can I use latex paint on top of a surface that was previously painted with oil paint?**
A **If you are switching to waterborne paints in your home after using oil paints in the past, you will have to prime everything you plan to paint.** If you don't, your new paint will not properly adhere to the old oil paint surface. Read the primer's label to check whether you need to lightly sand the surface before you prime it. Some new primers don't require sanding. If you are painting over water-based paint that is clean and in good shape, you can paint directly over your old paint—no need to prime.

Q **What is primer, and how do I use it?**
A **Primer prepares the surface for paint by stabilizing and sealing it.** It's not meant to cover the previous color and thus may look translucent and streaky. Don't try to block out the old color by applying a thick coat; just make sure you cover the surface evenly. The dried primer helps the next coat bond to the surface. Priming is often required; skipping this step is no shortcut to a good paint finish.

Q **How does the sun affect paint?**
A **Most of us apply sunscreen to protect our skin from harmful ultraviolet rays and wear sunglasses to reduce the strain on our eyes on bright days.** The sun affects our houses in similar ways; their exposed painted skin is particularly susceptible to heat and UV rays. The paint on the exterior of a house will eventually fade, peel, crack, and degrade from sun exposure. The inside of our house is not immune to the same dynamics. Modern houses often have UV-filtering windows to guard against the powerful negative effects of the sun.

Dark colors absorb heat—think of how hot the inside of a black car is on a summer day (there's a reason most cars with Arizona plates are white or silver). If you paint your house a dark color, it will absorb heat, which could be to your advantage in a cooler climate where the passive solar effect can help lower winter heating bills. But be aware that dark colors are susceptible to an accelerated aging process due to the heat absorption factor. This may be something to consider when planning your exterior painting project.

Q How can I avoid the toxic chemicals used in a lot of house paint?

A **Paint used to be high on the list of things most likely to contaminate your living environment, because it was filled with toxic solvents, chemicals, and lead.** Thankfully, modern paints have been reformulated to be much more environmentally friendly, due to greatly reduced or no VOCs (volatile organic compounds—the term used to describe the harmful vapors that are dispelled into the atmosphere as paint dries). Dry paint has no VOC level. VOCs can be very high in alkyd (oil) paints, which has led to a movement to regulate and even ban their use in residential envi-ronments. Every major paint company has created low- and no-VOC paints, and more are coming out all the time. I recommend checking *Consumer Reports* for up-to-the-minute reviews on the latest paint products.

Q My kids leave fingerprints all over my walls. Is there such a thing as washable paint?

A **Until recently, a higher-sheen paint, at the very least one with an eggshell finish, was the only way to go in high-traffic areas.** But paint technology has evolved. Now, thanks to new ceramic microbead technology, even matte-finish walls are washable. This is a huge advance, because you have the option of specifying a non-shiny paint anywhere.

Paint Sheen

Most of us know the difference between flat and high-gloss paint, but what about all the degrees of sheen in between? The shine level of paint can influence the end result every bit as much as the color. It's an important factor when selecting your palette. Most paint sellers have a sheen comparison chart available for you to look at as you decide which paint is best for your project. The sheens and nomenclature may vary somewhat by manufacturer, so ask the paint dealer to explain the distinctions by brand if necessary. The basic paint finishes are described below.

Flat

Flat finish paint has no shine at all. In fact, it often looks almost powdery. Because of its total lack of sheen, flat paint is the best finish for hiding surface imperfections. That's a big reason for using it on a ceiling. Many ceilings are not perfectly smooth because, let's face it, no one wants to work above their head with plaster and sandpaper for too long. And light rakes across a ceiling, catching every highlight (that is, imperfection) as it does. So if your goal is to focus attention on the color and decor and not on the less-than-perfect surface to be painted, go with the dullest sheen paint that's suitable: flat or matte for walls, eggshell for trim.

Matte

Matte-finish paint is often thought of as interchangeable with flat. But here is where the paint industry gets involved. The term *matte* was not used in the house paint industry until recently, when manufacturers sought to make distinctions among various products. Benjamin Moore uses the term *matte* to highlight their washable lowest-sheen paint. When dry, their matte finish is almost flat in appearance and has the added appeal of being resilient and mar-resistant if washed—a claim that basic flat-finish paint can't make. Bottom line: if you are looking for a washable flat-finish paint, it may be called *matte*.

Eggshell

Eggshell is a finish that is sometimes, not surprisingly, mistaken for a color. But when paint manufacturers use the term, they are referring to finish. Eggshell-finish paint has a very low sheen and is typically used on wall surfaces that are subjected to occasional moisture and moderate abuse. While not being overly shiny, it is easy to wipe clean. Hallways, kitchens, kids' rooms, and bathrooms are all great places to use eggshell-finish paint. I also like to use it on trim that is in poor shape, because it minimizes the flaws more than a higher-sheen paint.

Satin

Satin-finish paint is very popular for trim and cabinets. It has a sheen but is not glossy. It's easy to clean and durable. Some companies use the terms *low-luster* and *satin* interchangeably. I almost never use satin-finish paint on walls because it's too shiny for most rooms. But I usually specify it for woodwork and cabinets because it's lustrous and creates a pleasant contrast to matte or flat walls and ceilings.

Semigloss and High Gloss

Occasionally I'll use these high-sheen finishes for trim, depending on the project. It was once important to use a glossy paint in bathrooms and kitchens because any paint in a duller sheen would not resist moisture and couldn't be cleaned. But modern paints have improved to the point where even a very low-sheen paint is resilient enough for use just about anywhere, so high-sheen paints are much more about their look than their function. Light bounces off anything reflective, so the shinier the surface, the bigger the bounce. Our eyes are triggered by this bouncing light. We look at the bounce before we look at static, uneventful surfaces. I love high-gloss doors and floors for their glamour. And pristine trim or cabinets can also look chic with a high sheen. But remember, the higher the shine, the more visible every tiny speck, nick, and bump becomes. Surface prep becomes more critical as the sheen level of your paint increases.

The Painting Process

Most of us have either done some house painting ourselves or watched someone else paint. The novice method, performed every summer by college students, might be suitable for a rental apartment or a dorm room, but little else. It skips any kind of preparation and launches immediately into rolling on the paint. A professional painter spends far more time prepping than painting. Paint is a thin film that evenly covers the surface. It's not designed to fill or mask flaws and, in fact, does a good job of highlighting them. Paint should never be applied until after thorough surface preparation and priming have been completed. The better the prep, the better the paint looks and the longer it lasts.

1 Clear the Work Area and Protect Surfaces

Remove furnishings, window treatments, rugs, and so on. Cover anything in or near the work area with plastic, paper, or fabric drop cloths. If you need to tape something down, use painter's (blue) tape, which doesn't damage a surface when removed. If you are having the painters move your stuff, make sure that you or someone you trust is there to supervise and answer questions.

2 Set Up a Work Station

Create a staging area for paint and materials on a protected tabletop or on the floor in a well-protected area. Organize tools and materials and label each can of paint, using a permanent marker on tape, listing color, finish, and room. This is very helpful, especially if you have several people working on the site.

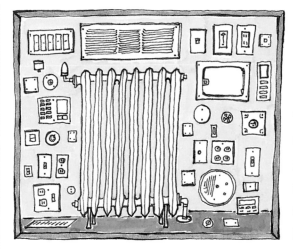

Tip: Use Ziploc bags for storing switch-plate covers and screws, plus any other small hardware.

3 Prep

Step One · Remove all loose paint and plaster from any surface to be painted. Use a five-in-one tool to scrape and pick loose paint and plaster away from the surface. Use appropriate scrapers and grades of sandpaper to smooth surfaces. For information on safety precautions regarding lead and debris removal for structures built before 1975, check the Environmental Protection Agency Web site (www.epa.gov/lead), which has valuable information regarding lead paint hazards and safe removal procedures. Always use gloves, dust masks, and eye protection and remove debris immediately.

Step Two · Clean dusty surfaces with a shop vacuum and/or damp cloths, then spot-prime any area that you plan on filling with plaster, Spackle, or caulk and allow to dry thoroughly.

Step Three · Fill areas with the proper material—caulk for seams, Spackle for most small surface voids, and joint compound alone or fortified with plaster for skimming larger surfaces. For trim, use wood filler, Bondo (an epoxy resin typically used for automotive body repair), or a product designed specifically for use on trim. Allow all filled areas to dry completely. Some deep repairs may require several applications of filler.

Step Four · Sand every surface by hand or with an electric sander. Pole sanders are excellent for large areas of wall and ceiling. Sponge sanding blocks and sandpaper are necessary for smaller, finer areas. Electric sanders can be useful on surfaces that have heavy paint buildup. The objective is to smooth the surface, not to remove layers of paint.

Step Five · Clean the project area completely. Use a shop vacuum, tack cloths, damp rags, et cetera, to remove all the dust from all the surfaces.

4 Prime

Always take the time to prime. Priming stabilizes a surface and prepares it for paint by promoting adhesion. Priming should be done with the proper applicator—brushes for trim and cutting in and rollers for walls and ceilings, or a spray gun for all surfaces in lieu of brushes and rollers. It

The Painter's Tool Kit

is not necessary to apply more than one coat of primer. Primer is for preparing the surface for paint, not for concealing what it's covering, so surfaces may look patchy after they are primed. This is normal. Once dry, all primed surfaces should be lightly sanded and wiped free of dust.

5 Paint

Finally, it's time to paint. A general rule when painting a room is to start at the top and work down—first ceiling, then trim, followed by walls. Always use the finest brushes and roller covers that the budget will allow. I prefer those made by Purdy, a professional painting tools manufacturer. A good brush makes your work go faster and look better; it's worth a few extra dollars. The wrong brush or roller sleeve can make even top-quality paint look bad, so ask a reputable paint dealer for assistance if you have doubts about which tools to buy.

Avoid thick roller covers because they leave a pronounced orange-peel texture on the surface. They should be used only over stucco or very rough surfaces. A short-napped roller sleeve is ideal for smooth surfaces because it deposits a thinner, more even paint film on the surface. It is always much better to take the time to apply two or even three coats than to risk a terrible-looking job by covering everything with one overly thick layer of paint.

Always follow the directions on the can. Paint companies do a tremendous amount of research for each product that they sell. Failure to follow directions could cause the product to fail or underperform. The manufacturer wants its product to perform properly just as much as you do.

TIP: Two thin coats are always better than one thick one. Don't skimp on labor.

A paint job will go far more smoothly if you keep the following items close at hand:

1 Scissors
So basic and necessary! Use to cut plastic sheeting, tape, and so forth.

2 Spackle
Keep a small container on hand for nail holes, small cracks, and dings in the surface of walls and trim. Spackle is not meant to cover large areas or fill deep holes, so use it for basic, superficial repairs. Always spot-prime over Spackled areas to make sure your paint adheres.

3 Small Spackle Knife
The perfect companion tool for Spackle. I prefer a one-inch flexible blade.

4 Five-in-One Tool
My favorite painting tool after the brush. I use it mostly to open paint cans, but it also scrapes the paint off roller sleeves, opens boxes, scrapes surfaces, loosens debris from cracks, and even works as a screwdriver to remove electrical plates.

5 Six-Inch Compound Blade
I use these wide blades to knock small imperfections off wall surfaces. They are also a good size for skim coating with plaster and joint compound.

6 Caulk and Caulk Gun
I am a big fan of caulk. Seams and cracks look like black lines and draw your eye to the dark little imperfections, so I like to get everything filled up and rendered invisible. Use a high-quality paintable product like twenty-five-year siliconized acrylic caulk.

7 Sanding Block
An update to sandpaper, a sanding block is a spongy block of foam coated with grit. It fits well in your gloved hand and, because it's foam, it conforms to the contours of molding. Get several grades—heavy for tough, bumpy surfaces; fine and medium for general use; extra-fine for smooth surfaces.

8 Nuisance Mask
Keeps out dust and debris but is not a replacement for fresh air.

9 Screwdrivers
Use them to remove all of the electrical plates and other hardware from the painting surfaces.

10 Painter's Tape
Often called blue tape, it will not damage the surfaces that it's applied to the way masking tape does.

11 Paint
Get the right paint for the job. Don't skimp; cheap paint will cost you in the long run.

12 Stir Stick
Usually handed out for free by the paint store. Stir your paint every hour to make sure it is properly mixed.

13 Nylon or Synthetic Bristle Trim Brush
I use a two-and-a-half-inch brush for just about everything—painting trim, cutting in walls and ceilings.

14 Nylon or Synthetic Bristle Sash Brush
This angled brush helps some people paint

straighter lines along the edges of window-panes and trim. I rarely use one because I am accustomed to using my trim brush for everything.

15 Roller Cage
I like a high-quality cage that holds the sleeve in place and doesn't squeak when it rolls.

16 Short-Nap Roller Sleeve
I use a quarter-inch nap sleeve for just about everything. It's deep enough to hold paint but not so deep that it leaves a big orange-peel texture.

17 Retractable Knife
Great for trimming tape and paper.

18 Pencil
Use it for making notes and putting paint numbers on the samples.

19 Notepad
You'll be happy you have it for taking notes and writing down color numbers.

20 Paint Sample Cards
Keep them around so that you have a record of the colors used.

21 Permanent Marker
Use it for putting names on cans and making wet paint signs—always important.

22 Paint Tray
Can be metal or plastic and comes in several sizes. Pick the size that corresponds to your roller cage.

Hiring a Painter

I'm one of those people who gets great satisfaction out of doing as many things as possible myself. And I actually love house painting. But for a big renovation or a large exterior project, even I would hire experienced painters. I've been recommending the same painter, Jonathan Teasdale, to all of my clients for years. He runs a very professional crew, is on the site working himself, keeps the job site spotlessly clean, and is polite, friendly, and accommodating. These are the qualities you should look for in a painter. Interview professionals who are insured, have been working in your area, and have references. If possible, go see a recently completed project, but at a minimum call the references and ask these questions:

· **Did the contractor complete the project on time and within budget?**
· **Was the contractor himself engaged and responsive?**
· **Was the site clean and well ventilated at all times?**
· **Was the crew professional and considerate?**
· **Did they use the appropriate supplies and paints?**
· **Were you completely satisfied with the job at the end?**

Estimates can vary widely, so get a written list of all the services the painter is bidding on and make certain that the scope of the project is well defined in advance. Don't just go for the lowest bid, unless you really feel that the bidder is competent and trustworthy, and you've seen evidence of the quality of his work.

Testing Colors

Think of testing as the ultimate shortcut to finding the right colors. Although the process may seem time-consuming and labor intensive, it's the only sure way to know whether a color will work before painting the whole room. Skipping this step means you could end up with an entire roomful of test color. Lucky you if it works, but if it doesn't you've invested way more time, money, and effort than testing would ever require.

I've been testing paint colors on project sites for years. If your painter or contractor balks at the process, beware—this is not a place to cut corners or save time. Even with professionals, I realized that I needed to develop a standard method for testing paint colors that would guarantee successful results. It's a good idea to explain your paint color testing plans to your contractor in advance, because it will take some additional time and paint. Here is a step-by-step outline of that process.

1 Purchase Sample Colors

Select your test colors from high-quality paint brands and order the smallest amount available per color. Some companies offer test-size containers, but most offer a quart-size can as the minimum size. While it may seem expensive to buy several quarts of paint, it is much cheaper than repainting an entire room if the color doesn't work out.

It's important that your carefully chosen sample colors not get lost in translation. To avoid the stress and uncertainty that paint color matching can cause, I recommend using the brand of paint that corresponds to the color chip you select. I'll sometimes use two or three brands of paint within one room. For me, it's all about the color. Painters often suggest having colors matched into a brand that they are familiar with (or get a discount on). This is not a good idea, for several reasons. Despite the confident claims of hardware stores and paint companies regarding the accuracy of their color-matching computers, the truth is that the "match" can be quite off. And when it comes to ordering more paint, you'll have no choice but to use the store that did the match, because it's the only source for what amounts to a one-of-a-kind formula. If you do choose to match one brand's color into another brand of paint, closely monitor the colors for accuracy. Test by tapping a dot of the new mix on the original paint chip and letting it dry completely. If the match is good, you should see no difference. The same goes for matching paint to a chip within a brand. Since most paint has its pigments added at the paint store, there is always the possibility of human error. Occasionally I'll get a container of paint that doesn't match another can of the same color. This is usually because of a miscalculation or the addition of an incorrect pigment during the mixing process. Return the incorrect mix for a redo or refund.

2 Determine the Best Locations for Test Patches

Color tests should be located at eye level and, if possible, on areas that can be seen from another room. If you are using sample boards, have someone hold them up in the right locations. This helps with sight lines, especially if you are changing colors from room to room.

If possible, paint samples next to a door or window frame because the straight

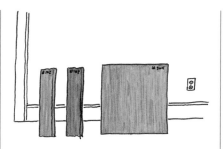

edge helps hold the color "still." I find that patches of color in the middle of walls do a distracting hovering thing, not to mention that the patch is competing with the surrounding wall color.

Your goal is to locate samples in the very best viewing spots, so take some time and figure out where your test colors should go before starting. If you are testing wall, ceiling, and trim colors, paint a corner of the room—a section of ceiling, some crown molding if you have it, and a portion of the walls below. This creates a snapshot of your scheme.

I often paint two-foot sections of loose trim boards for the trim color tests so I can bring them from room to room instead of painting trim repeatedly. This is particularly helpful if you plan on using the same trim color throughout all or most of your space.

TIP: If you don't have trim boards that match yours exactly, use a similar stock molding from the lumberyard that is approximately the same size as your trim.

3 Round One—Apply the Samples

I recommend testing paints directly on the actual surfaces to be painted, if possible. I've found it's just that much closer to the real thing than sample boards. But in the case of an already furnished house, where you don't want to risk wet paint spattering any surface, freestanding sample boards may be preferable. In addition, if you're considering a particular color for more than one location, a sample board is obviously handier. You should use something smooth, primed, stable, and as large as possible. I usually work on half-inch drywall board or eighth-inch Masonite that has been cut into two-foot squares. Don't use anything like poster board, which will warp when wet paint hits it. Warped paint samples are useless because they distort light, which distorts color.

When painting samples directly on the walls, some people mask the edges to make them neat and squared off. If you do this you may have to sand the edges of the samples before you apply the final coats of paint to the surface, because the taped line can create a tiny ridge of paint that can show up in different types of lighting. To avoid this, I make samples using a high-quality brush, and I fan out the edges, meaning that I brush the edges loosely and smooth the new paint into the surface. I still paint a square or rectangle, but with soft edges.

Your testing process should mirror the actual painting process. Whether you're painting the wall or a sample board, the surface should be primed. Once the primer is completely dry, the surface can receive its first coat of paint color. Recently there have been many changes in the paint industry, so paint cans often have new directions regarding drying times, coverage, and cleanup. Despite many manufacturers' claims regarding "one-coat coverage," you should apply two coats of paint to your samples. (One-coat coverage usually only refers to a color that is being applied over itself, effectively making it a two-coat finish.) The main issue regarding paint coats is that the color can be greatly affected by thin coverage. With too thin a coat, the primer layer can be read through the color, diluting and dulling the appearance. The most important thing you can do is to make sure that the paint is covering the surface completely. Two coats will usually do, three in certain circumstances such as deep colors, but total opaque coverage guarantees an accurate representation of the color.

TIP: I recommend using standard one-and-a-half-inch or two-inch paintbrushes or short-napped roller sleeves to apply the test colors. If you're taking a short painting break, keep the brush or roller from drying out between coats by sealing it in a plastic bag or with plastic wrap. If you won't be applying a second coat within a few hours, wash the brush with water between coats so it doesn't gum up.

4 Seeing Is Believing—Take a Break and Look at the Results

Once your test colors are dry and you've spent some time looking at them, take a break. If you have time, go get a coffee or take a walk, and come back with a fresh eye for color. Spend time looking at the colors in different light conditions at various times of day and night. If possible, look at your samples under the same lighting that you'll use in the finished room. Bring materials and fabric samples and hold them up with your tests. And listen to your instincts. Sometimes the right color is apparent right away. Don't talk yourself out of a color just because it presented itself too quickly. This process is about creating an environment that permits exactly that kind of response. Of course, this instant "perfect color" scenario may not happen at all, and you may have to think and look for a while until you decide. And there is always the possibility that none of the test colors will look appropriate. But even rejected colors are helpful because they steer us closer to colors that ultimately work. If no color makes it through round one, prime everything out and start again, keeping in mind that an entirely different color direction may be what's needed.

TIP: When selecting and testing colors in an environment where the floors are covered for protection from debris, I recommend lifting the paper or protective covering to expose the floor so that you can see your test colors with it.

5 Round Two—Test Additional Colors Until You Get It Right

If you need to do another round of testing, prime over all of your rejected colors, preserving any that are still in the running, and apply your second-round colors over the rejects.

6 Test Even Larger Samples to Squelch Uncertainty

Occasionally I will have painters cover an entire wall with the final color under consideration. I do this as an insurance policy. Our perception of color changes somewhat as the scale of the color field grows. If you have any reservations about your final choice, this is an additional step worth taking.

Recording and Preserving Your Colors

I always find it helpful to keep a careful record of the colors I've used on any project, because it is surprisingly easy to forget what you used and where. Having all of the information in one place is my insurance policy. Here is how I keep track.

1 Keep Records During the Color Selection Process

I use pencils to record color names, numbers, and information directly on the walls or on sample boards. Many people write on painter's tape and stick tags on the wall next to the colors, but I find this distracting. I do use tape to label the paint cans and lids, listing the room, surface, and color. Once a color is approved, I mark it as such directly on the wall or sample board. This helps avoid confusion.

2 Use a Notebook

Once you have selected all of your paint colors, it really pays to create a record of every color, room by room. My notebook is my bible and my lifeline. You should use one too, both for your own records and as a written summary that the painter or contractor can consult if a question arises. Here are some things to record:

- **Paint chip or Web link for more information**
- **Brand of paint used**
- **Type of mixture—alkyd or waterborne**
- **Finish—flat, matte, eggshell, pearl, satin, semigloss, or high gloss**
- **Method of application—brush, roller, spray, or combination**
- **Date of completion**
- **Contractor information**

I keep paper files and electronic files for each project. I often tuck fabric and wallpaper swatches in the paper file folders and attach before-and-after photographs to my electronic notes. There is no such thing as too much recorded information. You will be thrilled to be able to put your finger on just what you're looking for, especially when you've moved on to other projects.

3 Create a Touch-up Kit

At the end of a project I make touch-up kits for each room or area. I buy small mason jars and pour in leftover paint, filling them to the top if possible. Paint lasts longer if you don't leave much air space in the container. I make labels for both the lids and the jars, listing the brand, color number and name, finish, room, surface, and date. Everything is stored in a cool, dry place along with a printed copy of a master list of all the painted surfaces in the house, so if I need to do a touch-up, it's easy to put my hands on the right jar. I use a Q-tip to apply dots of paint to small nicks and scratches. For larger areas I use small brushes that I store with the touch-up kit.

Bibliography

Albers, Josef. *Interaction of Color.* New Haven: Yale University Press, 1963.

Ball, Philip. *Bright Earth: Art and the Invention of Color.* Chicago: University of Chicago Press, 2001.

Batchelor, David. *Chromophobia.* London: Reaktion Books Ltd., 2000.

Birren, Faber. *Color for Interiors: Historical and Modern.* New York: Whitney Library of Design, 1963.

Bristow, Ian C. *Architectural Colour in British Interiors, 1615–1840.* New Haven: Yale University Press, 1996.

———. *Interior House-Painting Colours and Technology, 1615–1840.* New Haven: Yale University Press, 1996.

Brusatin, Manlio. *A History of Colors.* Boston: Shambhala, 1983.

Crone, Robert A. *A History of Color: The Evolution of Theories of Lights and Colors.* Norwell, Mass.: Kluwer Academic Publishers, 1999.

Delamare, François, and Bernard Guineau. *Colors: The Story of Dyes and Pigments.* New York: Harry N. Abrams, 1999.

Finlay, Victoria. *Color: A Natural History of the Palette.* New York: Random House, 2002.

Gage, John. *Color and Culture: Practice and Meaning from Antiquity to Abstraction.* Berkeley: University of California Press, 1993.

———. *Color and Meaning: Art, Science, and Symbolism.* Berkeley: University of California Press, 1999.

———. *Color in Art.* London: Thames & Hudson, 2006.

Gass, William. *On Being Blue: A Philosophical Inquiry.* Boston: David R. Godine, 1976.

Goethe, Johann Wolfgang von. *Theory of Colours.* London: John Murray, 1840.

Ings, Simon. *A Natural History of Seeing: The Art and Science of Vision.* New York: W. W. Norton, 2007.

Itten, Johannes. *The Elements of Color.* New York: Van Nostrand Reinhold, 1970.

Linton, Harold. *Color in Architecture: Design Methods for Buildings, Interiors, and Urban Spaces.* New York: McGraw-Hill, 1999.

Moss, Roger W. *Century of Color: Exterior Decoration for American Buildings 1820–1920.* Watkins Glen, N.Y.: American Life Foundation, 1981.

———, ed. *Paint in America: The Colors of Historic Buildings.* Washington, D.C.: The Preservation Press, 1994.

Oliver, David. *Paint and Paper in Decoration.* New York: Rizzoli, 2007.

Riley, Charles A., II. *Color Codes: Modern Theories of Color in Philosophy, Painting and Architecture, Literature, Music, and Psychology.* Hanover, N.H.: University Press of New England, 1995.

Rompilla, Ethel. *Color for Interior Design.* New York: Harry N. Abrams, 2005.

Stromer, Klaus, ed. *Color Systems in Art and Science.* New York: Golden Artist Colors, 1999.

———. *Traditions and Colors.* New York: Golden Artist Colors, 2000.

Swirnoff, Lois. *The Color of Cities: An International Perspective.* New York: McGraw-Hill, 2000.

Theroux, Alexander. *The Primary Colors.* New York: Henry Holt, 1994.

———. *The Secondary Colors.* New York: Henry Holt, 1996.

Varichon, Anne. *Colors: What They Mean and How to Make Them.* New York: Harry N. Abrams, 2006.

Resources

Paint

AFM Safecoat
www.afmsafecoat.com
Behr
www.behr.com
Benjamin Moore & Co.
www.benjaminmoore.com
California Paints
www.californiapaints.com
C2 Paint
www.c2paint.com
Dunn-Edwards
www.dunnedwards.com
Earth Pigments
(pigments and lime)
www.earthpigments.com
Eve Ashcraft Color: The Essential Palette
(available from Fine Paints of Europe)
www.finepaintsofeurope.com
Farrow & Ball
www.farrow-ball.com
Glidden
www.gliddenprofessional.com
The Little Greene Paper and Paint
www.thelittlegreene.com
Mythic
www.mythicpaint.com
Pratt & Lambert
www.prattandlambert.com
Sherwin-Williams
www.sherwin-williams.com
Valspar
www.valspar.com

Historic Paint Colors and Renovation

www.oldhousecolors.com
Lots of information about palettes and paint
www.oldhouseweb.com
Comprehensive site for all things old
www.preservationnation.org
National Trust for Historic Preservation
www.welshcolor.com
Analysis of historic paint and wallpaper

Acknowledgments

The Right Color **is the result of many years of staring at walls, sifting through color chips, and having the good fortune of being surrounded by brilliant colleagues, clients, and friends who generously shared their thoughts, homes, time, and humor.**

I am indebted to Heather Smith MacIsaac, whose writing, editing, fabulous taste, wry sense of humor, and encouragement proved invaluable.

With endless gratitude, I also want to thank the following: Jeffrey W. Miller, who worked his magic finding many perfectly colored bits and pieces for my still-life color portraits and helped me brainstorm all along the way; William Abranowicz, for his remarkable generosity and beautiful photography; Martin Raffone, whose friendship and design genius both top out at 100 percent; Jack Wettling, architect and fine comrade, who never makes work feel like work; Gil Schafer, whose steadfast work ethic and attention to detail come close to rivaling his generosity; Victor Schrager, for making beautiful still-life photographs that made me look at the world differently; A. M. Homes, for her stalwart advice, unflagging support, and friendship; Anne Johnson, for suggesting that I might have a book inside just waiting to hatch; Victoria Tennant and Steve Martin, who handed me an enormous project and helped launch my career; Martha Stewart, for the opportunity of a lifetime at the right time; Jonathan Teasdale, who made painting thousands of walls more fun and interesting than it should have been; John Lahey and Fine Paints of Europe, for many years of support and their range of beautiful and dependable products; Michelle Andrews, Deborah Nevins, B. D. Wong, Derek and Martha Kellett, Cory Shields, Linda Rodin, Gene and Barbara Kohn, Lisa Lancaster, Jeffrey Stark, Sarah and Ozey Horton, Juliet Homes, and Courtney and Nick Stern, for generously sharing their projects and spaces; Lia Ronnen, Kevin Brainard, Ann Bramson, Jan Derevjanik, Sibylle Kazeroid, Nancy Murray, and the rest of the wonderful team at Artisan, for their support, skill, and ability to keep creating beautiful books; Megan Senior, Erica Ackerberg, and Robin Epstein, for assistance with photos and words; Jaime Wolf, Marilyn Lurie, and Joan Osofsky, for their advice and support; my grandparents Herbert and Martha Ashcraft, for their leap of faith as they sent me to art school; and my mother, Julie Jordan, with whom I wish I could share this book since it's her fault in the first place.

"There would be no blue without yellow and without orange."

—VINCENT VAN GOGH

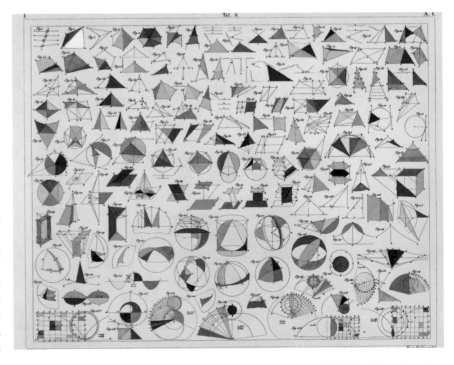